DEVELOPING CHRISTIAN LEADERSHIP

*Learning from the Greatest
Leader who ever lived*

TREVOR R. SUMMERLIN

WESTBOW
PRESS®
A DIVISION OF THOMAS NELSON
& ZONDERVAN

WestBow Press books may be ordered through booksellers or by contacting:

WestBow Press
A Division of Thomas Nelson & Zondervan
1663 Liberty Drive
Bloomington, IN 47403
www.westbowpress.com
844-714-3454

ISBN: 978-1-6642-8654-2 (sc)
ISBN: 978-1-6642-8655-9 (e)

Print information available on the last page.

WestBow Press rev. date: 02/14/2023

Contents

- To enable the production of shape, form and identity
- To enable people to see where they fit and how they relate to others
- To enable the protection of vulnerable parts
- To enable positive activity to take place

Acknowledgements

I have learned an enormous amount from many people in my life but I am particularly grateful to a select few who made a really significant impact on me during my early years. I am especially grateful to my parents from whom I seemed to inherit my mother's organisational ability and my father's patience. I owe a massive debt to the Rev A. E. Rushton, vicar of St Barnabas Church, Cambridge, where I worshipped and learned so much from the age of 7 until I was 19. I also gained such a lot from the officers of The Boys' Brigade at that time – Geoffrey Hewitson, Ron Meadows (Snr), and Derek Wilkin. Several other key people from the church were also incredibly important in my learning and development, especially Granville Hawkes, Brian Whittaker and Ronald S. Meadows. However, it was my lifelong friend and mentor, Rev John James, and his wife, who taught me how to apply the principles of The Bible in a much more exciting and dynamic way. Each one of these people has provided me with a solid grounding in the classical skills of a Biblical style of leadership by demonstrating, not just an attitude of service, but a complete willingness at all times to go out of their way to serve others.

I am extremely grateful to my wife Jan for her patient support and to our daughter Sara who collated the whole text into a transmittable document. Pete Wilkinson of Divi Engine produced the diagrams

Please note that throughout this book whenever the words 'he', 'him', 'his,' 'she', or 'her' have been used, no gender preference is intended.

The cover picture is used under licence from Shutterstock UK. It depicts a leader who is breaking new ground whilst tied to his followers for their mutual encouragement, support and protection. This arrangement builds trust and develops a strong bond between each of them so that no-one can inadvertently stray off track. It enables them to tackle serious and dangerous obstacles together as they follow a previously agreed route and stay in constant communication with each other.

About the Author

Leadership has played a vital role in the life of Trevor Summerlin since his ability in this respect was recognised at the age of seven. He was regularly appointed to leading roles through Junior and Secondary school and has occupied senior positions of leadership in a wide variety of different organisations and companies throughout most of his life.

He has held management positions in both Christian and secular companies, in Local Authority organisations, in Voluntary organisations and with National Bodies. He has worked in the Retail industry, the Manufacturing Industry and the Leisure Industry. He has experience throughout the UK, across Europe and around the USA with small companies as well as large business consortia. He has pioneered new opportunities, started new companies, launched new charities, been a manager, director, board member, chairman or consultant with many different organisations, and worked as a business management trainer.

He qualified as a Youth Leadership Trainer on three different levels in 1969, as a BASI ski instructor in 1979 and an English Ski Council Coach in 1980. He gained a Masters Degree from the University of Wales in 1997 through his examination of "Stress in Leadership" and qualified with the Family Mediators Association and the Legal Aid Board as a Family Law Mediator in 1999. He was appointed a Fellow of the Institute of Sales and Marketing Management in 1987 and a Fellow of the Institute for Leadership and Management in 2006. He is a Baptist Minister, a qualified Cognitive Psychotherapist and obtained a post graduate diploma in Coaching in 2005. He has been a lecturer, trainer and conference speaker in all aspects of therapeutic counselling and managed his own private practice as a Christian Psychotherapist and Supervisor for over 40 years. His motto for life is:

To serve God in Power as a Catalyst for Change.

Throughout his life he has been an enthusiastic sportsman, competing to a high level in many different sports but now, in addition to teaching The Bible, he and his wife spend their time ministering to others in the Christian faith, in Christian Counselling, in Writing and in trying to tame their garden in South Wales, UK.

PART ONE

ESSENTIAL FUNDAMENTALS FOR THE CHRISTIAN LEADER

enabled me to evaluate and learn from every situation I have encountered throughout every subsequent season of my life and it caused me to want to apply them every day as often as I could. I came to understand that good leadership is all about change, and change that is for the good, so as a result, I adopted this personal motto for my life:

To serve God in power as a catalyst for change.

There are, of course, many definitions of leadership and, because these can vary enormously, they have the potential to generate frustration, disappointment and disillusionment for followers. For example, there are likely to be great differences between what is considered to be good leadership in a secular organisation compared with what is seen to be desirable for good leadership in a Christian organisation or a church. The standards that are set in each case will depend either upon the world-view and management style that is adopted by each organisation or else it will simply be determined by the person in charge of the day-to-day affairs.

"The essential difference between Christian Leadership and other approaches which might be referred to as 'leadership' is that it has at its heart the spiritual growth and empowerment of individual people within the context of the development of the Kingdom of God" (Trevor Summerlin)

Although there are always going to be differences of style and approach regarding the practice of leadership, there are clearly many common factors which are related to the issues of how to make progress, how to develop, and how to change, whatever form these may take. Every organisation, activity or group of people will require some form of leadership if they are to function effectively and achieve their desired purpose. Whether they are professional or amateur, private or corporate, paid or unpaid, business or voluntary, secular or spiritual, formal or casual, in every sphere of life regardless of age or experience the quality of leadership will determine the levels of their success.

Leadership, by its very nature is not carried out in isolation because it will always involve working with other people. It is, therefore, a team activity which will incorporate many different elements such as: vision, recruitment, management, motivation, support, encouragement, planning and so on. The fundamental principles of good practice in leadership will always be needed regardless of the circumstances under which they are exercised. Therefore some of the most important questions to be addressed at this point are; - 1) where can we find the fundamental principles of good leadership?, 2) are there certain rules of leadership which should be followed?, 3) are people born as leaders or are they trained?, and 4) is it purely a matter for the person in charge to make all the choices and decisions?

Daniel Lancaster, in his book "Training Radical Leaders", maintains there are four essential qualities that are required to become an effective leader: Knowledge, Character, Skills and Motivation. He says –

"Without knowledge, wrong assumptions and misunderstandings will misdirect the leader. Without character, the leader will make moral and spiritual mistakes that hamper the mission. Without necessary skills, the leader will continuously reinvent the wheel or use outdated methods. Finally the leader with knowledge, character and skill but no motivation will care only for the status quo and preserving their own position" (Lancaster 2014).

As a Christian, I believe our manual on how to manage all aspects of human life is The Holy Bible and this is the place therefore where we can find God's strategies on how to conduct our lives in ways that will produce the best results. In other words, it tells us what actions and behaviours will be beneficial and successful both for ourselves and for others. Everyone knows that the best way to find out how to operate any technical piece of equipment is to consult the maker's instructions and many people will have had the experience of trying to put together a flat-pack piece of furniture without first attempting to understand the instructions – you might be lucky, or it might be disastrous.

For the purposes of this book therefore, regarding the principles of good leadership, I choose to draw on the depth of insight from our Maker that is recorded for us in the Scriptures. As a result of this, it will come as no surprise for you to discover also that I consider the greatest exponent of the principles of good leadership, which God has written in The Bible, to be

God's Son, Jesus Christ. He is, without any doubt in my mind, the greatest leader who ever lived because He is the only person who has a complete understanding of the way the human race has been designed to operate.

As we consider a wide variety of approaches and styles of leadership the overriding factor that must be taken into account, whether people accept this or not, is the fact that all humans are spiritual beings. It means that any attempt to ignore this is going to result in a process which, at best, can only ever be partially effective, or at worst is likely to be ineffective altogether. Christian Leadership therefore is that process which puts the spiritual element at the very centre of the leadership process, but this is only likely to be possible when the leader has a personal relationship with Jesus Christ and is a consistent student of Biblical principles.

This is not intended to be a book aimed exclusively at leaders of churches but is about how to apply the highest standards of leadership in any and every situation regardless of the environment in which it may be practised. Having said that, every church leader would do well to make themselves familiar with these principles and constantly seek to improve relationships with their creator in order to be of maximum help to the people they wish to lead. The real tragedy here is that the vast majority of churches and Christian organisations don't use a structured process to train or adequately prepare people to become leaders, but instead choose to rely on what they may call people's 'natural gifts and abilities', or even on the divine intervention of God.

2. Definitions

(i) Christian

Let me first of all explain more specifically what I mean when I use the word 'Christian'. I define a person as a Christian if they continue to acknowledge they have broken God's laws, that Jesus died to pay the full penalty for this sin and that there was no other way in God's sight by which they could be forgiven. Having acknowledged, confessed, and repented of this, they have invited Jesus into their life as Saviour and Lord, have received Him in the form of The Holy Spirit and now choose to allow

Him to continue His refining process by being determined to follow His principles and patterns of teaching as recorded in The Bible. The Christian Leader, therefore, is someone who is choosing to operate in every aspect of their role, to the best of their ability, according to the teaching patterns and principles of Jesus Christ.

To be able to do this effectively it will require the leader to be a person who studies The Bible on a regular basis and who is committed to serving others by putting what they learn into practice. The Christian element of leadership, above all else, demands the development of a servant heart. This is a willingness to go beyond the call of duty specifically for the benefit of others. In this way people seek to become more like Jesus who chose to lower Himself and become like us in order to lead us onto higher things. This principle is beautifully summed up in this extract from "The Servant King" by Graham Kendrick:

From heaven you came, helpless babe, entered our world Your glory veiled,
Not to serve but to serve, and give Your life that we might live.

This is our God, the Servant King, He calls us now to follow Him.
To bring our lives as a daily offering of worship to the Servant King.

Here in the garden of tears, my heavy load He chose to bear.
Hands that flung stars into space, to cruel nails surrendered.

So let us learn how to serve, and in our lives enthrone Him,
Each other's needs to prefer, for it is Christ we're serving.

To be Christian in leadership means being willing to take on a similar attitude of complete humility and personal self sacrifice for the benefit of others and to seek to meet their needs in preference to our own. As we come to terms with the person of Jesus, as recorded in The Bible, we begin to appreciate the challenge being presented to us, that to be a Christian Leader will involve an attitude of humble servanthood. This was spelled out specifically by the apostle Paul in his letter to the Philippian church:

"Do nothing from factional motives through contentiousness, strife, selfishness or for unworthy ends or prompted by conceit or empty arrogance. Instead, in the true spirit of humility and lowliness of mind, let each regard others as better than and superior to himself, thinking more highly of one another than you do of yourselves. Let each of you esteem, look upon, and be concerned for not merely his own interests, but also for the interests of others. Let this same attitude, purpose and humble mind be in you which was in Christ Jesus who, although being essentially one with God and in the form of God – possessing the fullness of the attributes which make Him God - He did not think this equality with God was a thing to be eagerly grasped or retained. Instead He stripped Himself of all privileges and rightful dignity so as to assume the guise of a servant, or slave, in that He became like men and was born a human being". (Philippians 2 verses 3 – 7 Amplified Bible)

One of the most significant principles to understand about Christian Leadership is to recognise that it is not to be confused with what the world understands as leadership. The Bible, in Romans chapter 12 and verse 2, reminds us that we are not to copy what the world does but to have a transformed view by allowing our minds to be renewed by The Holy Spirit. This means we must not allow the secular standards of leadership to creep into our work, even though many well-meaning leaders within the church may have chosen to do so, but we must be motivated and guided at all times by the leadership standards laid out for us in The Bible. What applies here to leadership can also be said to be relevant in terms of understanding authority:

Whether as a leader or as a follower, I believe we will never be able to understand Christian authority until we understand Christian Leadership.

The parables which Jesus spoke that are recorded in Luke chapter 15 about the lost sheep, the lost coin and the lost son, were not just given to explain about the qualities of Father God but are examples of the qualities that are an essential requirement for Christian Leadership, namely those of compassion, persistence and servanthood.

The current concept of Servant Leadership was developed by Robert K. Greenleaf between the late 1960s and early 1970s and was first published in his book *"Servant Leadership"* (1977). He identified it as a philosophy where the leader maintains an attitude of service towards the people who choose to be followers by sharing power and responsibility and by putting the needs of others first. He said that a key element was helping individuals develop and perform increasingly with a view to becoming potential leaders of the future, and he maintained that:

> *"the only authority deserving one's allegiance is that which is freely and knowingly granted by the led to the leader in response to, and in proportion to, the clearly evident servant stature of the leader"*
> (Greenleaf 1977 p10)

(ii) Leadership

I now want to look at the word 'leadership', which also needs a little explanation because it is frequently misunderstood and is often used inappropriately in the context of management. For the purposes of this book, we are not discussing management, which is primarily about how people handle things, but about leadership, which is primarily about how people handle people. What may sound obvious is that leadership is the act of leading, but leading can only be done when there is a clear attachment of the leader to a follower or a group of followers.

> *"Leadership, is to be committed to: a corporate concept of persons, the diversity of human gifts, covenantal relationships, lavish communications, including everyone, and believing that leadership is a condition of indebtedness"*
> (Max Depree 1989 p72)

Leadership is not a rank, but a role which cannot be performed externally or remotely because it needs to be in partnership with people who are in relationship together. Where no relationship exists, what might sometimes be referred to as leadership is more likely to be a form of dictatorship that will require constant attempts to persuade and manipulate people to commit themselves and get on board.

**A true leader is someone who spends his
time pouring himself into others.**

In The Bible, when Rehoboam sought advice from the elders of the nation of Israel (1 Kings 12 v 6-7) he was told "If today you will be a servant to these people and serve them and give them a favourable answer, they will always be your servants"

*Leadership is the active process of getting a group of people fully and willingly committed to new and sustainable courses of action that will meet mutually agreed objectives whilst maintaining and developing commonly held values.
(Adapted from Exeter University Centre for Leadership Studies)*

Another surprising fact about Leadership is that every single person, there are no exceptions here, is capable of leading. Leadership is neither the prerogative of the select few, nor of those who are already in positions of responsibility, but it is the ability of any person to use appropriately the gift that has been given them by God. However, like any other gift, it can lie dormant or be misused, but it has the potential to be trained and developed according to the circumstances in which people find themselves and in response to the opportunities which become available to them. How can we know that every person has the ability to be a leader? Because there can be no doubt that every person has the ability to lead someone astray and every Christian has the ability to lead someone to Jesus.

*"A leader is someone who makes something happen
that wouldn't have happened otherwise"*
(David M. Rubenstein 2020)

One of the key principles we find in The Bible is that everyone must be willing to submit to the leadership of someone else in their group from time to time (Ephesians 5 v 21) because leadership is about the appropriate exercise of a God-given gift. People are not born into leadership, and leadership should not be seen as some form of promotion. It should be the recognition of a person who has relevant gifts, skills, talents or abilities that are needed by a particular group of people, at a particular time, for a particular reason. As with every other gift, some people will naturally seem to be better at it than others, but because leadership is a gift from God (Romans 12 v 8) it needs to be nurtured and developed so it might bring glory and honour to Him by helping others.

"Leadership is about cultivating an environment that innovates and releases the missional imagination present among a community of God's people"
(Roxburgh & Romanuk 2020)

Leaders should never force themselves into position nor have any real desire to take control but should be motivated by a genuine desire to help other people achieve something with which they seem to be struggling. It should always be a reciprocal arrangement in which the leader is willing to receive as well as to give. The true essence of Christian Leadership is captured in this extract from a hymn by Richerd Gillard:

Brother, sister let me serve you, let me be as Christ to you.
Pray that I may have the grace to let you be my servant too.

We are pilgrims on a journey and companions on the road,
We are here to help each other walk the miles and bear the load.

I will weep when you are weeping, when you laugh I'll laugh with you
I will share your joy and sorrow 'til we've seen this journey through.

I will gain from being with you, grow in strength and Christ-like love
This is how we'll help each other rise to greater heights above.
(Adapted from Richard A. M. Gillard 1978)

One of the first examples in The Bible of the need for Godly leadership can be seen in the life of Moses. In Exodus chapter 3 and verse 10 God says to Moses that he is the man to <u>bring</u> the Israelites out of Egypt. Moses was commissioned by God to be their leader because he was one of them and understood them, so when the time came for him to hand over this role, this was his prayer:

"May The Lord, the God of all mankind appoint a man over this community to go out and to come in before them, one who will lead them out and bring them in so that The Lord's people will not be like sheep without a shepherd" (Numbers 27 v 16-17)

A similar concept was developed originally by James MacGregor Burns which he called Transformational Leadership. This was where the leader works with a group of followers to take them beyond their perceived capabilities and self interests. He said the Transformational Leader needed to be able to:

(i)   identify specific needs for change.
(ii)   develop and proclaim a clear vision.
(iii) outline the steps required to make such changes.
(iv)   bring about the changes through inspiration and influence.
       (Burns 1978)

Throughout this whole process the Transformational Leader would work with the members of the group, using mutually agreeable and beneficial activities, in order to create the maximum levels of practical involvement. This process was later adapted and expanded by Bernard M. Bass in 1985 when he identified 4 main components of leadership which he entitled:

1.   Inspirational Motivation
2.   Idealised Influence
3.   Intellectual Stimulation
4.   Individualised Consideration.

Some people believe that a further development of Transformational Leadership would be possible if it was implemented by a charismatic leader, that is, someone who has a natural ability to inspire, motivate, and arouse a positive emotional response in their followers. However, a charismatic quality could not provide such a development on its own, since it could contain many potential weaknesses, as Ray Williams pointed out in his article "Beware the Dark Side of Charismatic Leadership". https://raywilliams.ca posted on 28th April 2019.

Jamie Turner, an online blogger of leadership issues, published "The

Four Pillars of Leadership" which he identified as: Mentoring, Marketing, Mindset, & Management. He later added a further four: Accountability, Respect, Responsibility and Servanthood. These ideas were further developed by Dr Ronald E. Riggio who is the Henry R. Kravis Professor of Leadership and Organisational Psychology at Claremont McKenna College. His Four Foundational Pillars of Leadership are:

1. Be a Positive (and Ethical) Role Model
2. Be Inspirational, Optimistic and Align Values with Goals
3. Be Challenging but with Support
4. Be Listening and Genuinely Concerned for your followers.
(www.psychologytoday.com posted 24th March 2009)

It seems to be clear from these examples that for any style of leadership to be effective it must be conducted by someone who belongs to the group of people he is leading so he is taking people with him rather than simply issuing instructions for others to follow. I believe this is what has the potential to produce the greatest levels of satisfaction and success for any leader. In our exploration of what constitutes Christian Leadership, we can see this clearly demonstrated in the life of Jesus. He spent years living alongside His disciples to train and prepare them before releasing them into active service on their own, and you can sense the joy and excitement He experienced (Luke 10 v21) as they were praising God after returning from one of their ventures.

All the principles regarding Christian Leadership that are identified in this book can be applied by any person working with any group of people in any situation. They are intended to be guidelines that will awaken a desire within every person who is in a leadership role, or who is considering taking up such a position. My hope is that every leader or potential leader who reads this book might be willing to find a way of applying Biblical principles of Christian Leadership as they undertake their own leadership challenges.

Never-the-less, I do want to stress that anyone who is involved in the leadership of a church or a Christian organisation would also do well to heed these principles. However, I hope that all kinds of leaders everywhere will take these principles on board because they work, and they work because they are part of God's plan and heart-felt desire for us to be successful, which He has outlined in His manual for life, The Bible.

PART 2

ESSENTIAL UNDERSTANDINGS FOR THE CHRISTIAN LEADER

Essential Understandings for the Christian Leader

In this section we are going to consider a variety of different approaches that might be used to identify a philosophy for Christian leadership. Whilst I am aware that these can be adapted and used with any kind of project, regardless of whether it is Christian or not, we will be emphasising their application with regard to Christian principles. This will only be a sample selection because there are an innumerable number of possibilities, but the intention here is to stimulate creative thinking and provide a few suggestions which may not be very obvious to lots of people.

> **A philosophy for leadership is a personal point of view about a system of values and attitudes that can be applied to the process of leading a group of people so that everyone can understand and appreciate the overall framework within which the work is being carried out.**

Whatever philosophy for Christian Leadership is adopted, it is likely to reflect the personality of the individual leader, but it should really be tailored to meet the needs of the group being led as well as to conform to any wider vision and objectives that exist from the parent organisation. To be implemented correctly, any philosophy will involve the application of a range of genuine people-skills, and we look at these in some depth in Part 4.

The idea of having a philosophy for leadership is to provide a really helpful way of gauging the process of helping to maintain the direction and momentum of a group. In fact, without any awareness of a particular philosophy it is much easier for the leader (and the group as a whole) to lose focus and go off at tangents which can result in a constant process of 'fire-fighting' or leadership by default. Such a 'fly-by-the-seat-of-your-pants' attitude, where people are making it up as they go along, is not conducive to good leadership and really has no part in true Christian Leadership. That is not to say that spontaneity should be restricted, nor that guidance from The Holy Spirit is not important, but that these need to find their place within an identifiable God-given framework.

Our foundation for this section is drawn from the idea that the Christian faith is not an ad-hoc series of beliefs that have been cobbled together on the spur of the moment, but a carefully structured programme for spiritual growth and maturity by building relationships with people and with God. In this section we review a few of the approaches which could be used advantageously by any Christian leader.

1. A General Philosophy for Christian Leadership

- Everyone Connected
- Everyone Contributing
- Everyone Contagious

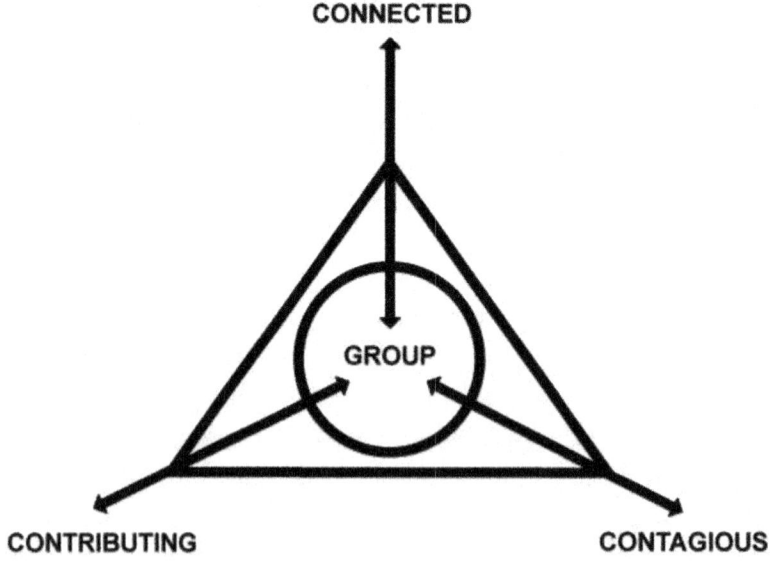

Diagram No1 A General Philosophy

This is a general approach to Christian Leadership which can be used in many different kinds of situations. So often we tend to work on the assumption that people must reach a certain standard of commitment before they can be allowed to take any active part in the organisation. As a consequence we can miss the opportunity to get people involved as a means of helping them make a commitment. Rather than adopting the outdated traditional approach of insisting that people must be believers before they are allowed to be involved in anything, one church pioneered the strategy for people to "Belong before they Believe and Believe before they Behave". This enabled many non-church people to find faith and to learn about the values and standards of behaviour that were being encouraged within the church before they were invited to make a formal decision to join. As a result of adopting this approach their work and effectiveness in the community grew rapidly and their numbers increased accordingly.

(i) Everyone Connected

Two of the most significant aspects about leadership, which really need to be in place before any leadership activity begins, are (a) the need for every person in the group to feel that they are positively connected, and (b) for any outsiders who want to be involved, to get connected. It is going to be quite impossible to effectively lead a group of people who are scattered in their thinking and attitudes or where people are not starting at the same point, or have any real sense of common agreement.

This principle is often overlooked because of the enthusiasm on the part of the leader to get things moving as quickly as possible and to do this by excluding anyone who isn't already connected to the group. He may also assume that everyone who appears to be part of the group is equally connected and enthusiastic about the tasks that lie ahead. It is an easy mistake for any leader to make, to assume that everyone is ready to move and to imagine that any problems that may arise can be resolved as things move along. However, issues like this which are not dealt with from the outset are likely to develop into more serious issues further down the line.

People generally need to know that the leader really wants them to belong to the group and that they are important to him. They need to feel wanted and significant and those who don't have such an assurance are likely to be the stragglers who can hold back the progress of the whole group. Unfortunately this part of the process always takes time and effort because it involves the leader meeting people individually to discuss and listen to their views about the direction of the group. It involves allowing people to freely express their thoughts and opinions and to know that the leader has heard and taken notice of these as he works out the strategy.

Getting people on board with the project will require the leader to outline the development of a clear vision and strategy for the group whilst still being willing to modify, adapt, and change this in the light of people's comments. People need to know what it is they are being asked to connect with and the leader may need to go out of his way to ensure people really understand and agree with this and that they wish to be fully committed to it. There will need to be some clear goals established so that each person can see the potential benefits, both for themselves as well as for the group, because vague goals will result in loose connections.

Jesus spoke about the importance of refusing to abandon any individual who may be sidetracked or waylaid (Matthew 18 v 12). He makes clear that the responsibility of the leader is to be willing to go out of his way in order to bring them back into the group, even if it means they need to be carried for a while. Many leaders might not see this as their responsibility and could easily choose to delegate this job to someone else, but the reality is that this is a vital role for the leader to be seen to be fulfilling.

Demonstrating practical care and concern for individuals, even if they are deliberately choosing to separate themselves, is an absolutely necessary function of Christian leadership. However, in order to avoid people being coerced into things they have no wish to be a part of, the leader must be able to assess each person's overall intention. This will convey a strong message that each person is important and underlines the principle that there is greater strength and unity when everyone is connected.

(ii) Everyone Contributing

Once a strong connection has been established with everyone and people know that they really do belong, the next phase in this philosophy is to ensure that everyone actually contributes something to the work of the group. This is not just about giving people the opportunity, but about ensuring that no-one is overlooked or squeezed out but is actively encouraged to participate. There will often be strong people who may be gifted or experienced in some way and it would be easy to allow such people to dominate the group so this will require sensitive management.

There will be a natural temptation for any leader to want to shut down anyone who tries to regularly be at the forefront of everything. Some leaders may feel their position to be threatened by such people or they may tolerate such behaviour by trying to ignore it and just focus on encouraging the quieter ones to come forward. Either way, this can convey the wrong message unless it is made absolutely clear that everyone, without exception, does have a part to play and that their skills and gifts are wanted, valued, and will be used.

The Bible repeatedly draws our attention to the fact that every individual person has been gifted by God and that we all have a responsibility to recognise this and encourage, even make space for, people to use their gifts. It can require time and effort to coach the more reticent people to become active whilst still maintaining the interest of the more talented people, but this is where genuine leadership skills come into play. Less skilled leaders will generally opt out of this responsibility because it requires a real compassion for the underdog and may result in time-consuming adjustments needing to be made to the whole programme.

Good Christian Leadership will always seek to ensure that a balance is maintained at all times so that every person can be actively involved. Much more time is usually needed to encourage those who may lack confidence, and are shy or fearful, to help them find their place in the group (Romans 15 v 1 – 6). This will prove to be time well spent in the long run and will pay dividends for the group as a whole.

"Without involvement there is no commitment"
(Stephen Covey)

It requires the leader to assess each person's commitment to the group and its ideals to ensure that every contribution people make is moving the group towards its objectives. Sometimes the level of a person's commitment can only be gauged by what they are willing to contribute and if a clear strategy is not already in place it can create uncertainty and fragment the group by allowing struggles for superiority to develop. The leader must deal with such issues positively so it will encourage everyone to be more committed to the group and to know that every person's valuable contribution will be respected.

(iii) Everyone Contagious

One of the most exhilarating things about leadership is to see the people with whom you are working become genuinely excited about the tasks in which they are involved. Some people think it is the role of the leader to generate this kind of excitement within the group but it can neither be manufactured nor demanded. For it to be real it has to come from the individuals and be completely spontaneous. Only then is it likely to become infectious so that it spreads to others in the group and beyond.

The idea of being contagious is that you want everyone to catch the same vision. When someone is genuinely excited about something, it is often quickly picked up by others and can quickly change the atmosphere of the whole group. Spirits get lifted, fun and pleasure return, a positive attitude develops, people are more supportive of one another, everything becomes lighter and easier so that things get done more efficiently, the work becomes so much more enjoyable and even people previously on the fringes get drawn into the action.

There is no doubt that individuals as well as groups function at their best when there is an atmosphere of excitement about the work being undertaken. When the disciples returned to Jesus after being sent out to preach the Kingdom and heal the sick, they were filled with joy (Luke 10 v 17), and it is likely that all 72 of them were actively involved, regardless of their background. This would have had a phenomenal effect on the original twelve disciples as well as on the whole community and greatly contributed to the spread of the gospel at that time.

Someone once said "The Christian gospel has to be caught, not taught"

It is quite common for the leader to feel excited about the work he is helping the group produce and have a desire for this to rub off onto others in the group, but the real excitement only occurs for everyone when it happens without any prompting from the leader. Certainly the leader should be setting the trend and will want to generate enthusiasm by his example, but when this is caught by people in the group and it spreads exponentially the effect can be quite dramatic.

It only begins when people are able to experience a real sense of freedom to express their gifts within some clearly defined boundaries. Too much control will inhibit the way people are able to use their gifts so they need to know how exercising their gifts will be helping the group achieve some of its objectives. This principle is now widely accepted as fundamental in bringing up children:

Boundaries with no freedom produces frustration, whereas freedom with no boundaries produces anarchy.

The leader should be instrumental in this process by assessing the level of enthusiasm each member of the group has towards the corporate objectives rather than simply to their own objectives. This sort of enthusiasm is usually a genuine indication of the likelihood of an outbreak of contagion and the contagious attitude of a few can increase the potential for growing levels of enthusiasm amongst the whole group. When the group begins to change in this way it is likely to create an impression on those who may be benefitting from the work as well as on others who are outside the group.

2. A Foundational Philosophy for Christian Leadership

One of the most influential writers regarding the principles of management and good leadership is Stephen R. Covey. In his book *'First Things First'* he identified four human needs that are fundamental to experiencing fulfilment in life and he captured the essence of these by using the phrase, "to live, to love, to learn, and to leave a legacy". These are principles which should be applied, not only by everyone who wishes to be a leader, but by every person regardless of their roles or responsibilities. Stephen went on to say:

> *"The need to live is our physical need for such things as clothing, food, shelter, economic well-being and health. The need to love is our social need to relate to other people, to belong, to love, and to be loved. The need to learn is our*

> *mental need to develop and to grow. The need to leave a legacy is our spiritual need to have a sense of meaning, purpose, personal congruence and contribution".* (Covey 1994 p45)

He further maintained that if any one of these needs were to remain unmet, it will become a black hole which will have an effect upon each of the other areas and seriously reduce the quality of that person's life by demanding more attention and sapping their energy.

There is an uncanny resemblance here between what Stephen Covey talks about and what Selwyn Hughes identified as the five areas of human functioning (Kalmier 2011). Following Selwyn's time working alongside Dr Larry Crabb in America he was prompted to develop his 5 Circle Model as a means of enabling counsellors to help people face and manage their problematic issues. He began by recognising that human beings are made up of Spirit, Soul and Body, and he then added to this the common understanding that the Soul consists of Mind, Will and Emotions.

As a result of this, he identified five specific areas of human functioning as follows: the body which he called the Physical dimension, the feelings he labelled as the Emotional dimension, the ability to exercise our will and to make choices he called the Volitional dimension, the mind he called the Rational dimension, and the transpersonal element he called the Spiritual dimension.

Although Selwyn developed this model especially for the purposes of training counsellors, it clearly has the potential to be used much more widely. For example, I have found this model to be very successful when used as a prompt and a guide in management, business and leadership training programmes. Therefore, for the purposes of this book, and as a means of developing a foundational philosophy for Christian Leadership, I have chosen to adapt and combine the two theories of Stephen Covey and Selwyn Hughes into the following philosophy:

(i)   Know how to Live – Physical – Experience life in all its fullness
(ii) Know how to Love – Emotional – Experience the full range of feelings
(iii) Know how to Learn – Rational – Experience the thrill of new discovery

(iv)   Know how to Lead – Volitional – Experience development opportunities

(v)   Know how to Leave – Spiritual – Experience the power of purpose.

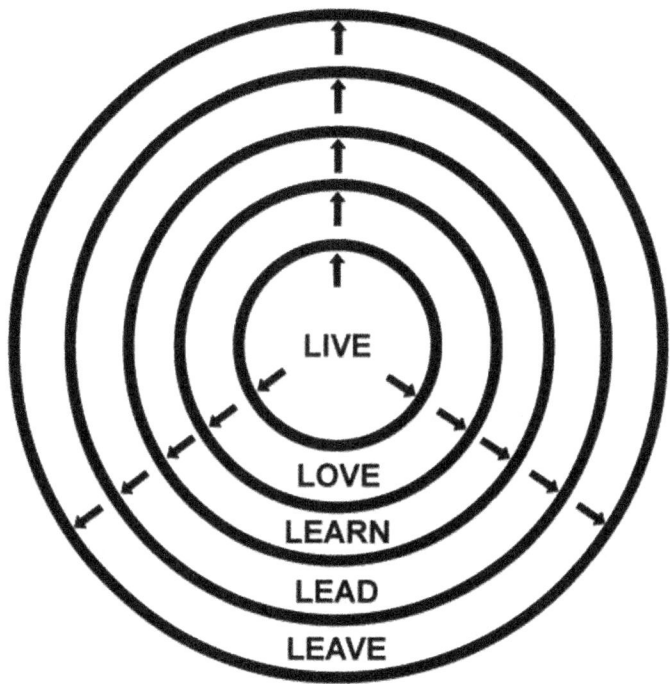

LIVE

LOVE

LEARN

LEAD

LEAVE

Diagram No2 A Foundational Philosophy

Adapted from Selwyn Hughes (1990) and Stephen Covey (1994)

It is essential for the life and activities of the Christian Leader to fully embrace each of these areas if he is to be effective in helping others to move forward in a balanced and dynamic manner. This will involve being able to give encouragement to others to be bold as well as giving them a strategy to face and deal with any problems or blockages which might hinder their progress. So in each of these areas we are looking to establish principles which the leader should apply in his own life as well as ways in which he should seek to encourage these in the lives of his followers.

(i) Know how to Live

The physical dimension is all about learning to live in as healthy, fulfilling and rewarding a manner possible and to deal with any physical problems as soon as they occur. Consulting a doctor or a medical professional should be a normal response to any physical aches, pains or injuries we may have, but it is surprising how many people choose to live with their problems instead of seeking appropriate advice. They don't seem to realise that every difficulty in the physical dimension is going to have a negative impact on every other dimension of their life.

Choosing a healthy lifestyle, which involves care about our diet as well as our exercise regime, will enable us to function more effectively emotionally, rationally, and spiritually and it will help us make more appropriate choices in these areas too. This means we can set ourselves up to experience life with more vitality, excitement and enjoyment. It is not unusual for problems we may be facing in other areas of our life to have their root in unresolved physical issues. For example, common issues such as Stress, Anxiety, Depression and Fear can often be the result of an underlying physical problem.

However, this is not just about dealing with the negative issues but about choosing to live life to the full by taking every opportunity to exercise our gifts, abilities, talents and skills in ways that will benefit others and, at the same time, help us to grow. It is about the giving of ourselves to others instead of allowing an attitude of self gratification to dominate our lives. We must not let the worldly standards of instant reward and self aggrandizement dictate our actions.

For Jesus, experiencing life in all its fullness meant being obedient to everything The Father was telling Him - and nothing else. Learning to live by a higher power (ie; to be guided by God), can be a real challenge, but it is a vital ingredient for every Christian. The only way for us to fully know real purpose, fulfilment and satisfaction in this life is by choosing to live in a positive and obedient relationship with Jesus. This is what will enable us to add a real sense of meaning to our existence here on earth and will give us the genuine joy of seeing others get blessed.

(ii) Know how to Love

It is a common belief among leaders that they should at all times maintain an air of detachment from what is happening around them and especially from the people they are leading. Some are even embarrassed to show any sign of their emotions or to demonstrate any real sense of compassion or to get involved in any celebration of the success of others. This usually comes from a selfish desire to reinforce their position as leader whereas, in fact, it has exactly the opposite effect. It shows a lack of connection with the people in the group, demonstrates a fear that others might see the real person, and generally indicates a superior need to be appreciated.

Learning how to love is essentially a process of learning how to be honest and give of one's self to others. We must be willing to admit to and accept our feelings, whatever they are, and not be afraid to show them whenever it is appropriate. Our willingness to demonstrate love and commitment towards others is the one thing that will increase the likelihood of others showing their love and commitment towards us. The spiritual principle here is that of both giving and receiving. If anyone wants to receive love, they must first of all be willing to give love to others. People who feel unable to love others inadvertently give the impression that they themselves are unlovable.

Similarly, when leaders give the impression that they are completely unmoved by circumstances around them by being unwilling to show any emotion, it reduces the likelihood that people will feel able to share their own emotional experiences with them. There is a balance required here because dissolving into floods of tears at the drop of a hat is clearly not going to be helpful, whereas an appropriate show of emotion can reveal a sense of empathy and demonstrate a caring attitude towards others.

When Jesus showed His emotions by being 'deeply moved' and weeping at the tomb of Lazarus (John 11 v 33-36), all the people could see how much He loved them. Although the love Jesus had for Lazarus and his two sisters was not in doubt, I believe He was weeping not so much for Lazarus, because He knew He was going to raise him from the dead, but for all the people who didn't yet understand who He was and didn't know what He could do for them.

It is the willingness to try to understand what is going on for others in the group that creates an atmosphere of trust and predisposes people to be more likely to open up and share their hearts. This can happen spontaneously when the leader shows a genuine love for those in the group, along with the patience to really listen to them. The main difficulty here is that this will involve the leader spending time with individual people rather than forging ahead with his plans, but it is the only way to be sure he is taking people with him, and he can only be a leader if people are following.

Knowing how to love will also require the leader to demonstrate several other important qualities such as being reliable, keeping commitments, not breaking confidentiality, and sharing responsibilities and plans. Where an atmosphere of secrecy exists it will always be difficult to build trust and this will result in the leader needing to spend much time trying to convince the group about his ideas and then attempting to motivate people to back him.

The demonstration of knowing how to love is the practical activity of showing love to other people regardless of whether they deserve it or not. This is not to be regarded as a 'soft' quality because this not an emotional sloppy kind of love. It is being able to love when the going gets tough and this is a response to knowing the way Jesus loves us – through the good times as well as the bad. It is captured in the words of this Jimmy and Carol Owens' song from 1997:

> "God forgave my sin in Jesus name, I've been born again in Jesus name.
> In Jesus name I come to you, to share His love as He told me to.
>
> Freely, freely you have received, freely, freely give,
> Go in My name and because you believe, others will know that I live".

(iii) Know how to Learn

A person's willingness to keep learning is a clear indication of their desire to be a good leader. Those who give the impression they have nothing to learn do not make good leaders. Good leaders are committed to continually developing their understanding and by seeking to learn from every situation they identify themselves more readily with the members of their group. Christian Leadership must be a continuous process of learning and of never getting to the end of that process. However, this is not simply about learning new skills or studying academic journals or even about becoming more accomplished at the work being undertaken.

The key here is to be willing to learn from every situation whether good, bad, or indifferent, and for this to become such an intrinsic part of the Christian Leader's mentality that it marks him out as being different to most other people. An attitude of mind like this can only be developed from a complete sense of trust in the sovereignty of Almighty God and it comes from being an on-going student of The Bible. Only when we have no doubts in our mind about God's ability to bring something good out of every situation will it be possible for us to know for certain that there is something for us to learn in every situation.

This element requires us to choose to bring our minds into line with the Word of God, even when we believe we know better and even when the whole world seems to be saying something different. When we do this, The Lord opens to us a whole treasure chest of new and exciting things for us to discover which can be as much about ourselves as about other people. It requires a high level of honesty and patience to be able to grow and mature from it but, once mastered, it will enable us to begin to face every day and every challenge with a new sense of excitement and adventure.

Stephen Covey, in his book *"First Things First",* outlined a principle which he calls 'The Law of The Farm' (Covey 1994). This is the realisation that circumstances and people move and change according to God's timings rather than our own. Stephen explains that the law of the farm is a steady gradual process which cannot be hurried and where everything happens in its season. We are living in a world where people want everything faster, quicker, or even instantly and because people have no time to appreciate gradual process they are losing the ability to wait and to ponder. The growing interest in techniques such as Mindfulness, Yoga and various forms of Meditation bear this out.

Many people have a tendency to leave things to the last minute and then rush to get everything completed. They are relying on a rush of adrenalin to help them get through, but the law of the farm says it's no good waiting until August to plant your seeds and then expecting to get a harvest in September. There is a God given timing to certain things and we attempt to override this at our peril. When we are prepared to allow God's timings to take precedence in our lives we will have greater opportunities to learn so much more. Stephen puts it like this:

> *"We find out there is a difference between succeeding in the social system and succeeding in the development of the mind – the ability to think analytically and creatively at deep levels of abstraction, the ability to communicate orally and in writing, the ability to cross borders, to rise above outmoded practices and solve problems in newer, better ways"* (Covey 1994).

We are able to embark upon a process of discovery that can fill us with a level of excitement like no other. We begin to be caught up with the genuine thrill of the realisation that there is so much that we don't know, about everything, and that the process of discovery and learning can be one of the most enjoyable and never ending aspects of Christian Leadership.

(iv) Know how to Lead

My firm belief is that every person, regardless of age or background, is capable of being a leader but there are several major stumbling blocks that can prevent this from happening. The individuals around some people may consider them to be unsuitable for leadership and not be willing to give them any opportunities, a person may consider themselves to not have the necessary qualities for leadership or, comparing themselves with others a person may feel inferior and shy away from opportunities for leadership. However, we all have responsibility to notice the gifts people have and to encourage them by giving them opportunities to use them (Romans 12 v 4-8).

An important part of being a Christian Leader is the role of mentoring. Everyone in any position of leadership should be taking on the responsibility to train and mentor other people. The role of leadership is not just about going somewhere or achieving something, but about preparing other people (Ephesians 4 v 11-12) to become servant leaders for the benefit of the individuals, the group, and the organisation.

The real skill of leadership is the development of more leaders, not the creation of more followers.

However, although every person is capable of leading, not many people actually learn how to do it effectively. Even amongst those who do take a leading role, many believe they have a natural ability for the job and see no need to receive any form of training. Such an arrogant approach really marks them out as those who are unsuitable for leadership, but popular opinion or selfishness will often keep them in position (Luke 6 v 39).

How foolish it would be for someone who has a natural gift for playing the piano to think they could simply step onto the stage and perform with an orchestra without many hours of dedicated practice and training. Every single gift we possess, even though it is God-given, is going to need honing and refining if we are to achieve the highest standards that will bring glory and honour to God. Many gifted people have failed to make the grade because of a lack of either the right kind of coaching and training or the dedication to rigorous practice. So we must be careful never to assume that raw talent, however good it appears, needs no further training.

The additional challenge concerning Christian leadership is that you never get to the end of the learning and developing process. There are always new things, new opportunities, new approaches, new circumstances, new difficulties to be faced, new revelation to be received and new wisdom to be acquired. Of course, many of these will be dependent upon the environment in which the leader is working and therefore this must be taken into account when any training or coaching is being considered but even this should not be seen as a substitute for the regular on-going study of the principles recorded in The Bible.

The main point I wish to reinforce here is that appropriate training and coaching can help to remove many of the frustrations that come to a leader and can dramatically reduce the incidence of stress and burnout which wreck the lives of so many leaders. Leaders are frequently caught in the middle of a dilemma where the people on one side don't really appreciate the problems being faced and the people on the other side don't really understand the advantages that can be achieved. The pressure this can produce is often underestimated until the knock-on effects become unavoidable and the damage it can cause to personal health and relationships is sometimes irretrievable.

Leading in any environment should be an exciting, invigorating, joy-filled experience that produces amazing rewards both for the leader and all those participating. It should be a constant process of exploring ways of increasing effectiveness so that weariness will be reduced to a bare minimum.

(v) Know how to Leave

One aspect of leadership that is often completely overlooked is the skill of knowing when and how to move on. It is possible for us to become so entrenched in the role of leading, including the hassles and the knock-backs, that we can lose sight of the fact that all positions of leadership are for a season. We should, therefore, always be aiming to work ourselves out of the job by preparing others to go further than we are able. This principle reduces the likelihood of stagnation, both for ourselves and for those who are followers, by maintaining a dynamic sense of purpose.

For the Christian leader it can only be possible to maintain a dynamic sense of purpose if he maintains a daily communication with The Lord. Hearing His voice, knowing His promptings and walking in close fellowship with Him is the only way we will be able to respond to His guidance and continue to experience the power and dynamic of His purpose. Without this, our work can become stale and laborious and the job of maintaining a good relationship with the people we lead is likely to become much more difficult.

However, we must be careful not to go to the other extreme where we are continually reminding everyone that we could leave at any moment.

This would just create a sense of insecurity for the group which can undermine any trust that has been established. Finding a balance in this respect will require wisdom, sensitivity to the people in the group, and a willingness to be obedient to what God is saying. Our spiritual connection is what makes this possible and so our private life becomes a massive influence on the way in which we handle this element.

Stephen Convey believes this element should be about the legacy we leave behind, which should be primarily a spiritual one. I agree that we should always aim to leave a spiritual legacy but we often don't realise that this is only achieved when we choose to pour ourselves wholeheartedly into our followers. The reality of our legacy will actually be determined by the way we have conducted ourselves in each of the previous four elements rather than whether we achieved what everyone expected from us.

The legacy of the Christian Leader will be the people we leave behind when it is time for us to move on. What will determine whether our actions have been honouring to God or merely some form of self aggrandisement is the quality of the lives we have been able to influence, the standard of the followers we have recruited, and the effectiveness and dedication of the leaders we have equipped.

3. A Structural Philosophy for Christian Leadership

- To enable the production of shape, form and identity for the work
- To enable people to see where they fit and how they relate to others
- To enable the protection of the more vulnerable parts of the group
- To enable the positive activity of growth and movement to take place.

In this section, which may actually be very appropriate for Churches and Christian organisations, we will look at the necessity for Christian Leadership to provide a solid framework for growth, development and achievement. In this context we will consider the human skeleton as a God-given example of how a strong, stable structure, even though it is absolutely vital, actually has no need to be seen. Without a skeleton, human beings would be just a blob on the ground, unable to move or do anything. Similarly, without a definite structure, any organisation will be equally ineffective and without a strong, stable framework any attempts at leadership will become a never ending struggle of frustration and disappointment.

For leadership to be effective, every leader and every follower must be aware of the structure within which they are working. From a Christian point of view we have only one head, the person of Jesus Christ, everyone else is part of the body. There is no hierarchy here and The Bible makes it perfectly clear that we are all equal and that nobody should consider themselves any better (or any worse) than anyone else (Romans 3 v 23). Just like the bones of the skeleton, if Christian leaders are to do their job effectively, they must be firmly connected to one another and to the head, whilst retaining the flexibility to perform the functions for which they are designed.

Christian Leadership should function a bit like the tiny cogs, wheels and springs in an old fashioned pocket watch – each one having a specific role yet working in perfect harmony for the benefit of the other parts.

Throughout the New Testament of The Bible Christian believers are frequently referred to as 'a body', but we can also take this to apply to any group of people who are working together, hence we can make a comparison between the human skeleton and Christian Leadership. The skeleton is made up of a wide variety of shapes and sizes of bones because they do not all do the same job. Nevertheless, whilst having quite different functions, there are great similarities in their role, for example; they provide shape, they provide protection and they enable movement. They don't do the work of the body but their job is to enable it to happen.

There are those who think The Bible outlines certain leadership roles as being of greater importance than others. They may draw attention to the words of Ephesians chapter 4 and see the role of Apostles, Prophets, Evangelists, Pastors and Teachers as a kind of hierarchy, whereas in reality, verses12 and 13 explain clearly that the job of each of these roles is not to do all the work but to be equipping others to do the work. This is reinforced in verse 16 where we are told that the body "grows and builds itself up in love as <u>each part</u> does its work". With this in mind, we are firstly going to consider how an examination of the 33 bones in the human spine might give us a better understanding of how these particular leadership roles might be seen to function together.

To link their significance as Christian leaders, the groups of bones in the spinal column could be identified as follows:

- 7 Cervical   - Apostles   - The Sent Ones
- 12 Thoracic   - Prophets   - The Seers
- 5 Lumbar   - Evangelists   - The Searchers
- 5 Sacrum   - Pastors   - The Shepherds
- 4 Coccyx   - Teachers   - The Scholars

THE HUMNAN SPINAL COLUMN

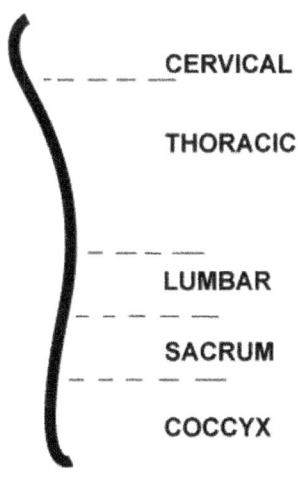

CERVICAL

THORACIC

LUMBAR

SACRUM

COCCYX

Diagram No3 A Structural Philosophy

Collectively they provide complete protection for the spinal cord without interfering with it in any way yet allowing it access to every area of the body. The spinal cord itself could be likened to the role of intercessors who continually relay vital messages back and forth from the head and need to be protected. The cartilages, or discs, which interleave and protect each of the vertebrae, remind us of the great importance of surrounding every aspect of the work in prayer. This is the lubrication that allows great flexibility and enables everything to function smoothly and without any friction.

Let us now consider each of these groups of vertebrae in more detail:

(i) 7 Cervical (Apostles)

> These vertebrae are the closest to the head and support the head. They help the body to maintain its equilibrium; they enable all-round vision and peripheral awareness. They help to maintain a right relationship between the body and the head. Apostles are the pioneers of the kingdom of God who, by maintaining a good connection to 'the head', are able to develop plans and create structure. They are the visionary planters and builders who break new ground. They are specifically commissioned to go into uncharted territory. They are explorers and adventurers who lay positive foundations, share vision and develop strategies that will benefit the body and achieve previously agreed objectives. There is a great need in every organisation to identify the people who are gifted in this way.

(ii) 12 Thoracic (Prophets)

> This is the largest group of vertebrae. They hold and support those who provide protection and covering for vital organs of the body (the ribcage). They provide support and a direct link to the Pectoral Girdle (the ability to be doing). Prophets are the 'seers', those who hear from God and speak out His word clearly and boldly. They give shape to the body and provide guidance and direction in a way that will give protection to vulnerable parts. Their work frequently includes both the foretelling (prediction) and the forth-telling (preaching) of the word of God. Every organisation needs people who are sensitive and can relate to external pressures yet are able to remain strong and protective at all times.

(iii) 5 Lumbar (Evangelists)

This group of vertebrae provide much needed flexibility and strength to the spinal column and create a strong link between the 'Going' and 'Doing' functions of the body. Evangelists are like the preachers who continually search for opportunities to present their message in attractive ways that will hold the attention of their hearers and draw them into the kingdom. They are the 'work-horses' of any organisation and are instrumental in its ability to be achieving its objectives.

(iv) 5 Sacrum (Pastors)

These vertebrae fuse together in adulthood to provide strength and balance to the body and protection for the reproductive organs. They connect to the Pelvic Girdle (the ability to walk and stand upright). They can be likened to church Pastors who provide stability with care and attention to the needs of the body. They are the shepherds who seek to provide the very best of welfare, food and shelter by meeting the needs of people in the organisation whilst protecting their ability to grow.

(v) 4 Coccyx (Teachers)

This is the smallest group of vertebrae, but together with the Sacrum they form the second largest group. They are also fused together to provide a similar benefit to the body of increased stability. Teachers are the scholars who seek to explain and educate the body with an accurate balance of learning. They are gifted at explaining things in logical and constructive ways so that people can fully appreciate and understand. They provide the teaching and training that will enable development and growth for the organisation.

It is clear that whilst some people have a specific gift in one or more of these roles, it must be recognised that some elements of each of these roles are built into every Christian believer. Everyone is capable of pioneering something for the kingdom of God or of speaking boldly and confidently to someone about the word of God. Everyone is able to seek out someone who is in need in order to help them or to show a struggling person how to draw on the resources which God has freely made available.

Everyone is also able to draw another person under their wing to support, encourage and prepare them to be able to stand on their own. The spinal column is a picture of a team of enablers whose job is to release the rest of the body (including other leaders) into their specific areas of gifting for the benefit of the whole body. In this analogy if we consider the whole human skeleton as Leaders, we can see how every bone plays a vital part in enabling the body to move and perform effectively.

In Christian Leadership no single bone (leader) is more important than any other or any other part of the body. Together leaders create the shape of the body, they enable each other to fulfil their function, they provide necessary protection to the vulnerable parts, and they facilitate the 'going' and 'doing' for which the body has been designed. However, whilst the body may receive external acknowledgement of its successes, like the skeleton, the Christian leader must be willing to remain completely out of sight.

4. A Spiritual Philosophy for Christian Leadership

- Understanding the Person and Working of The Holy Spirit - to Convict you (John 16 v 18)

- Understanding the Purpose and Calling of The Holy Spirit - to Change you (2 Corinthians 3 v 18)

- Understanding the Power and Anointing of The Holy Spirit - to Clothe you (Luke 24 v 49)

THE WORK OF THE HOLY SPIRIT

Diagram No4 A Spiritual Philosophy

Many people may question whether Christian Leadership should be referred to as a spiritual philosophy and whether it is appropriate to place any emphasis at all on the roles of The Holy Spirit but, because we recognise that people are primarily spiritual beings living in physical bodies, it would be a grave dereliction of duty to ignore this vital principle of leadership. Christian Leadership is much more than just doing the practical things and so a keen awareness of the work of The Holy Spirit is going to be essential if the work is to be successful. This approach therefore, is not just significant for leaders, but is relevant for every person in all walks of life.

Every aspect of the Christian faith is brought into focus by the movement and activity of The Holy Spirit. From the very beginning the whole of creation was brought into being by The Holy Spirit (Genesis 1 v 2) and the human spirit was formed as God breathed His Spirit into man (Genesis 2 v 7). Jesus was conceived by The Holy Spirit (Matthew 1 v 20), He was baptised with the Spirit (Luke 3 v 22), He was daily led by the Spirit (Luke 4 v 1), cast out evil spirits by the Spirit (Matthew 12 v 28), was offered up in sacrifice through the Spirit, and was raised from the dead by the Spirit (Romans 11 v 8).

The Bible makes it clear that the same Spirit that worked in Jesus works also in us and if we are being led by the Spirit we are God's children (Romans 8 v 14). We are born-again by the Spirit (John 3 v 5), we are anointed and empowered by the Spirit (Romans 8 v 9), we are being transformed into the likeness of Jesus by the Spirit (2 Corinthians 3 v 18) and are guided daily by the Spirit (John 16 v 13). The qualities of Jesus are given to us through the fruits of the Spirit (Galatians 5 v 22-23), and we become channels of His supernatural power by exercising the gifts of the

Spirit (1 Corinthians 12 v 7). It is the Spirit that prompts us to respond to God and comes to live within us to motivate us (Ephesians 3 v 16). It is the law of the Spirit that delivers us from the law of sin and death (Romans 8 v 2) and it is the Spirit that brings back to our memory the things God has already revealed to us (John 14 v 26). God communicates directly to us through the Spirit and reveals Himself to us through the Spirit (Romans 8 v 14). Furthermore, He has provided the sword of the Spirit – The Word of God – to enable us to stand against the strategies of the evil one (Ephesians 6 v 17).

If we are to function at all as Christian Leaders in this world, we simply cannot do this without The Holy Spirit.

The role of the Christian Leader therefore must incorporate each of these aspects in his own life as well as recognising each of these roles in the life of his followers.

(i) Understanding the Person and Working of The Holy Spirit

The Holy Spirit is God, He is the third person of the Trinity, He is the power and personality of the living God, and He is the presence of God in the world today. He is continually at work in and around everything we do. He makes the presence of God a reality for us and reminds us that we are children of God.

The Holy Spirit can speak directly into our human spirit and this enables God to reveal His plans and purposes to us on a daily basis. He is the one who will never leave us or forsake us. He comforts us in times of distress and gives us His joy to celebrate our successes. He is present wherever we go so we can talk to Him at any second of the day. Jesus said "He lives with you" (John 14 v 17) which means, even when we don't realise it, He is right beside us.

His role in being beside us is to dig us in the ribs occasionally and prompt us to respond to Him. This part of His job is to convict us (John 16 v 8) or challenge us about our life choices by speaking truth to us. This is His external role and it requires us to be honest with ourselves in order that we might receive His Divine Guidance (John 16 v 13) because He wants nothing but the very best for us.

A number of symbols are used in The Bible to represent The Holy Spirit and each of these helps us understand a little more about His character and qualities. When He is referred to as a Dove and as Breath it reminds us of His gentleness and that He can come to us very softly in a personal and intimate way. He is the perfect gentleman and does not attempt to draw any attention to Himself or to embarrass us in any way.

He is sometimes referred to by the symbols of Oil or Water. These remind us of His ability to come to us smoothly, without any harshness or discomfort. Oil also speaks to us of His plentiful provision and Water speaks of His refreshing power. The symbols of Wind and Fire are used to convey His awesome, supernatural power which can be seen both as His ability to strengthen and empower us as well as an indication of His future wrath and judgement (Hebrews 12 v 29).

The Christian Leader must constantly be sensitive to possible ways in which The Holy Spirit may be convicting individual followers in his group. This will usually be the beginning of significant changes for that person and they may need real support and encouragement during such a time. The Christian Leader must also be constantly alert to the promptings and challenges of Holy Spirit in his own life and take the time to process these appropriately.

(ii) Understanding the Purpose and Calling of The Holy Spirit

Once The Holy Spirit resides within us, He aims to bring the personal qualities of Jesus directly into our lives. These are known as 'The Fruits of The Spirit' and are recorded in Galatians chapter 5 verses 22 and 23. The purpose of these are to begin our transformation into the likeness of Jesus (2 Corinthians 3 v 18). However, He only comes into our lives at our invitation (John 14 v 17) and can only change us to the degree we are willing to be changed.

The Holy Spirit calls us to be different from the people of the world around us by allowing Him to change us from the inside so that we might be able to demonstrate the reality of God's presence in everyday life. He is the one who is able to reveal the plans and purposes God has for us

(Ephesians 2 v 10) and make us a channel of blessing to others. He can speak to us in a wide variety of ways including through dreams, visions, and pictures but also by giving us the words to say or highlighting to us what God has said in The Bible.

The fruits of The Spirit are planted within us when The Holy Spirit comes into our lives. This begins when we accept Jesus as our Saviour and Lord and we invite Him to take up residence in our hearts. The fruits then begin to grow and, as we feed and nurture them, they will eventually blossom and produce real evidence of God's transforming power. They enable us to begin to respond to the world around us in the same way that Jesus would without trying to gratify our own selfish desires.

The qualities of Jesus, or the fruits of The Spirit, are; Love, Joy, Peace, Patience, Kindness, Goodness, Faithfulness, Gentleness and Self Control (Galatians 5 v 22-23). These qualities gradually grow and develop within us as we choose to follow the teachings of Jesus and through these The Holy Spirit bears witness with our human spirit that we are indeed being fashioned into the children of God (Romans 8 v 16). This is an on-going process that continues throughout our entire life so it requires wisdom on the part of the Christian Leader to recognise this, both in himself and in others.

(iii) Understanding the Power and Anointing of The Holy Spirit

The Holy Spirit is the supernatural power of God that He released into the world on the day of Pentecost for the benefit of all mankind. He had promised this 400 years earlier (Acts 2 v 16-21) and, as Jesus explained (John 14 v 26), The Holy Spirit would be the one who would guide, counsel and empower His followers from that time on. This is the same Holy Spirit who worked in creating the world, the same Holy Spirit who worked in the life of Jesus, and the same Holy Spirit who empowered the disciples of Jesus to be His witnesses throughout the whole world.

Jesus referred to The Holy Spirit coming 'upon' His followers in this way as a baptism (Acts 1 v 5 and v 8). This experience is quite different to what happens when The Holy Spirit comes into our lives at conversion with the purpose of changing us. This anointing is to clothe us with His power (Luke 24 v 49) specifically for the benefit of other people and it requires an act of total surrender on our part in order that we might become channels of His supernatural gifts.

The difference between The Holy Spirit coming into our lives at conversion and receiving the baptism of The Holy Spirit is a bit like the difference between drinking a cup of water and falling into a swimming pool: the first is a controlled choice whereas the second is complete abandonment, the first is an act of the will, the second is an act of God, the first is about changing us, the second is about changing the world.

The supernatural, or the 'beyond natural' gifts of The Holy Spirit are: Wisdom, Knowledge, Faith, Healings, Miracles, Prophecy, Discernment, Tongues, and the Interpretation of Tongues (1 Corinthians 12 v 8-10). We can learn to move in this supernatural power of The Holy Spirit as we daily commit ourselves to walk with Jesus in obedience, not relying on our physical senses but trusting in His guidance and direction in everything we do.

The Christian Leader has a responsibility to allow The Holy Spirit to work in this manner and not to keep getting in His way. It requires the need to specifically make space for individuals in his group to develop towards spiritual maturity by exercising their gifts in an environment where they can receive encouragement and correction and training. As they grow in stature they will need to be released to go further than the leader is able to take them.

5. A Practical Philosophy for Christian Leadership

To be able to provide effective leadership to any group of people it is extremely important to begin to understand the gifts and abilities of each member of the group. Even when this is achieved, the greatest challenge is then to find ways of getting each person to use their qualities, without restricting the qualities of anyone else in the group, so that each person achieves a high level of satisfaction regarding the role they play. However, it is also especially important in this approach for the leader to recognise his own role in relation to others in the group.

The concept of people having specific roles to play in the work of a team or group was first developed in 1981 by Dr Meredith Belbin in his book *"Managing Teams: Why they Succeed or Fail"*. His theory was that if people were allocated jobs according to their abilities and interests it would result in vastly improved job satisfaction for the workers and this would produce much greater levels of efficiency and achievement for their organisations. He identified nine distinct roles as follows:

(i) Shapers
(ii) Co-ordinators
(iii) Plants
(iv) Resource Investigators
(v) Monitor Evaluators
(vi) Implementers
(vii) Team Workers
(viii) Completer Finishers
(ix) Specialists

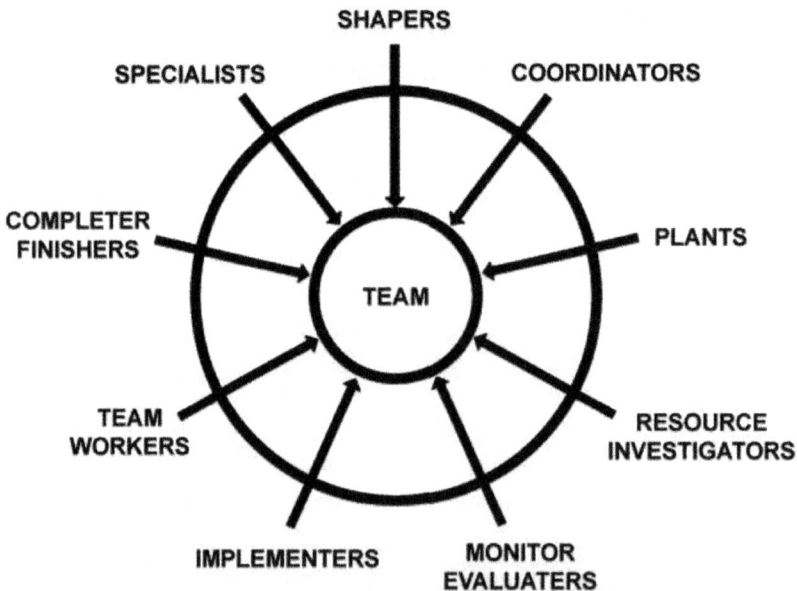

Diagram No5 A Practical Philosophy

Adapted From Dr M Belbin (1981)

Shapers are people with drive and courage who will demonstrate determination to overcome any obstacles. They tend to thrive on pressure and enjoy challenges. They possess a dynamic attitude that helps to shape the group, to work out its priorities and create structure. They are full of energy but can be a bit headstrong. They are prone to offend people and can be easily provoked.

Co-ordinators are those people who are able to organise the progress of the group by helping to maintain momentum and direction. They demonstrate a maturity and confidence by being cool, calm and collected but can sometimes appear too laid back. They are sensitive to the needs and the abilities of others and try to include everyone. They are willing to delegate to others but, on occasions, can be seen as being manipulative.

Plants have the ability to generate new ideas in unorthodox ways. They are problem solvers who are creative and are imaginative thinkers. Their free thinking often brings fresh insight into difficult matters but they have a tendency to become isolated from others in the group and are frequently misunderstood. They are likely to ignore some minor matters and can become totally preoccupied with their own agenda so as to fail to communicate with others effectively.

Resource Investigators are those who love exploring and developing new resources through their wide range of contacts. They are generally outgoing and enthusiastic about all they do but are sometimes over-optimistic. They are generally good communicators but their relaxed attitude and inquisitive nature means that they can easily become bored once the excitement of new things begins to die down.

Monitor Evaluators have the ability to make shrewd judgements. Their clear thinking enables them to weigh ideas, analyse problems and evaluate suggestions with calm accuracy. They tend to look at the bigger picture before making their own measured response. They have a tendency to be lacking in personal drive and have little ability to inspire others. They can sometimes become hyper-critical and stand-offish.

Implementers are usually hard working and well organised. They possess practical skills, are efficient and reliable. They have the ability to translate ideas into action by seeing what needs to be done and organising the work appropriately. They have a tendency to be inflexible and can be slow to respond to new opportunities by being resistant to change.

Team Workers do not like any form of friction or conflict and tend to avoid these at all costs. They are good listeners who are diplomatic, sociable and completely non-threatening. They are co-operative with great awareness and sensitivity to the needs of others. They are inclusive encouragers who can keep the morale of the group high but can be quite indecisive in critical situations.

Completer Finishers are conscientious with a high level of accuracy. They are careful and thorough about everything but can be relied upon to get the job done and to meet agreed targets. They are independent and single minded but sometimes have a perfectionist mentality. They are inclined to be over-concerned with detail and can sometimes lose sight of the bigger picture. They have a tendency to become possessive.

Specialists are those who are able to bring a high level of detailed knowledge to the group, which is often in short supply. They are strongly dedicated but within a narrow sphere of focus. They tend to be self sufficient and often impatient with the weaknesses and failings of others. They are likely to get frustrated when there is a lack of attention to technical details.

Utilising this approach to Christian Leadership can dramatically improve the levels of harmony and efficiency within any group, but the Christian Leader may need to spend a lot of time helping each person recognise their own qualities as well as to appreciate those of others. In this approach, the Christian leader must take one of these roles and choose to defer to each of the others. His main work therefore, will involve helping everyone to see how all these different roles can work together to achieve the objectives of the group.

If this can be achieved, it can transform the relationships and greatly increase the levels of harmony within the group. This sense of shared responsibility will generally improve the opportunities for progress to be made. Although these are the major positive qualities Belbin identified, we must also be aware that there are a great many negative qualities which could surface as major distractions and must be handled appropriately when they do. Here are a few of these:

The Theorist is someone who has their head in the clouds so they have little contact with the ground. They often have very detailed knowledge but lack any practical application.

The Dreamer possesses a great sense of vision, often in great detail, but this is 'pie-in-the-sky' thinking and frequently out of touch with reality.

The Complainer is totally negative in every way by finding fault with every suggestion and idea. They are often disillusioned and can be hurtful towards people who have very fixed views or opinions.

The Historian is a 'done-it-all-before' person who will explain what went wrong last time and all the reasons why it couldn't possibly work now.

The Know-it-All believes everything will be easy, so wants to race ahead all the time. They have no patience with planning but believe they already know exactly what needs to be done. They can be difficult to hold back and frequently leave a mess in their wake.

The Unrealist has ideas that are a hundred times bigger than what is really going to be possible. They often criticise others for being narrow minded and for their lack of faith and commitment.

The Defeatist can always prove why something will never work. They can produce 'evidence' of failures from the past and logical reasons why things will never be successful.

The Disappointer will always volunteer to help but can never be relied upon. They tend to let you down at the last minute, often for very plausible reasons.

The Spectator finds it impossible to commit to anything. They seem to be interested in what is going on by wanting to be around the action but never get involved.

There are many other negative roles the Christian Leader may come across. Each of these will require time and attention to be managed effectively in order to minimise the amount of disruption to the group.

6. A Developmental Philosophy for Christian Leadership

One approach to leadership which has become quite well known in recent years is the process of group, or team, development which was identified by psychologist Bruce Tuckman in his 1965 paper "Developmental Sequence in Small Groups". He identified four stages of development and labelled them; Forming, Storming, Norming and Performing. Tuckman later added a fifth stage which he called Adjourning, or Mourning, to indicate the demise or disbanding of the group at the end of a project. However, I have replaced this with my own fifth stage which indicates that the group may need to be completely restructured if it is to continue.

(i)   Forming
(ii)   Storming
(iii)   Norming
(iv)   Performing
(v)   Re-Forming

5. RE-FORMING

4. PERFORMING

3. NORMING

2. STORMING

1. FORMING

Diagram No6 A Developmental Philosophy

Adapted from Bruce Tuckman (1965)

The end of one aspect of a project does not necessarily mean the end of the group as a whole, so I call my fifth stage Re-forming. The Christian Leader may be able to take advantage of these stages in the management and leadership of his group by applying this model to his work. It could help individuals recognise what needs to happen for the group and for the project to move forward, and to see what part they may need to play to bring this about.

(i) Forming

This is the stage where people are being brought together for a common purpose but where their uncertainty and insecurity may often be a limiting factor. Strong and sensitive leadership is required at this point to identify a clear vision and a strong strategy. It is important for the leader not to force these onto the group but to draw these from the individual members whilst identifying what their personal needs and objectives are. The group need to get to know each other and establish a bond that will enable them to support each other if the work is to progress.

(ii) Storming

This can be the most challenging stage for the Christian Leader because it usually involves handling objections and alternative ideas without marginalising people. Internal conflicts will often surface over individual responsibilities and ways of doing things. There may be challenges over the leadership of the group and questions about the purpose and process that has been outlined, but groups that stagnate at this point will eventually become dysfunctional. Doubts and fears are commonplace at this stage causing people to struggle to see how they will fit in and whether anything can actually be achieved. Clear lines of communication need to be established quickly that will remove any anxiety and allow every person to know their views are being heard. The objectives for the group need to be discussed and agreed, and these must take into account the need for individuals to achieve their own objectives. This is a time for building trust and ensuring that everyone knows they really do belong and have a part to play.

(iii) Norming

Once any problems have been resolved people will be able to settle into their roles and, keeping their focus on the main objectives, will be able to undertake the tasks of the group. Internal relationships should now allow the free flow of information and feedback that will benefit everyone in the group. The group should now be gelling together effectively and be encouraging one another to take responsibility and be fully committed to the work. The Christian leader will be having open discussions with people individually and corporately on a regular basis to ensure that everyone is kept fully in the picture and to ensure that any problems are being quickly and appropriately dealt with. Individual skills are recognised and any weaknesses or gaps in the expertise of the group are being recognised and filled.

(iv) Performing

The group is now in full flow and the group begins to reach its true potential by achieving their objectives and meeting their targets. The evidence of this becomes its own encouragement for the group, making it easier to delegate responsibilities and share the workload. Standards of operation begin to improve and become easier and everyone is able to witness something of their own personal development taking place. In this stage the Christian Leader needs to arrange for successes to be celebrated and rewards to be given whenever this is appropriate. Everyone should be complimented on their work and encouraged to grow from the experience.

(v) Re-Forming

To maintain success for any group it will always mean embracing an attitude of change. At this stage roles need to be adjusted, objectives need to be re-drawn, vision and mission statements need to be updated, new agreements need to be put in place, responsibilities need to be reviewed, new people and new skills need to be incorporated into the group and people need to be allowed to move on to other realms of service whenever this is appropriate. Christian Leadership will often involve a long term commitment to certain objectives, so it will always require a high level of flexibility to facilitate these kinds of adjustments.

This model is not intended to be a concept which is rigidly adhered to but one which is applied as the group goes about its work. It is envisaged that groups might move back and forth through the stages as various issues surface and changes in the group or the project become apparent. The Christian leader will need to be constantly aware of the necessity of balancing the overall progress of the project with the goals of the individual members of the group because both of these should be of equal importance.

7. A Progressive Philosophy for Christian Leadership

(i) Create Real Team
(ii) Supply Compelling Direction
(iii) Develop Enabling Structure
(iv) Ensure Supportive Content
(v) Provide Expert Coaching/Mentoring

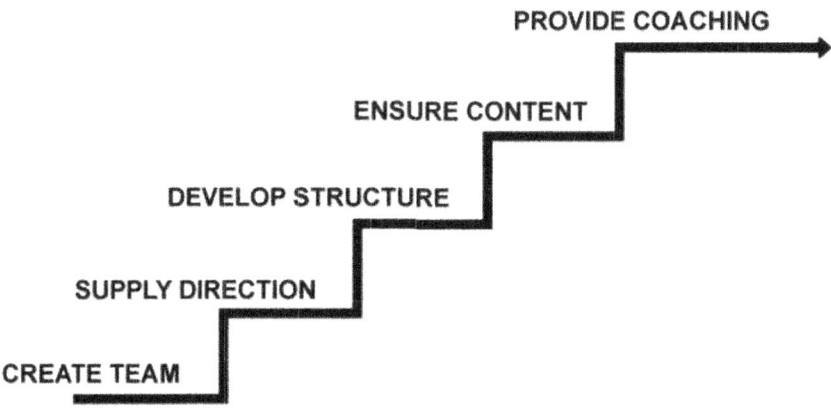

Diagram No7 A Progressive Philosophy
Adapted from Richard Hackman (2002)

This is adapted from the work of Richard Hackman who developed the "Five Factor Model" (2002) in which he outlined the need for members of any team or group to find meaning and satisfaction from their work.

(i) The creation of a real sense of team is the responsibility of the Christian Leader by drawing people together into a strong, stable relationship. This will necessitate the establishment of certain boundaries so that everyone knows who is part of the group and who is not and people can see there will be a role for each of them to play. Groups will always function best when each person can understand the role they are being asked to play and can see how this will be contributing to the overall work of the group.

(ii) A compelling sense of direction must be developed by the Christian Leader in consultation with the members of the group and in harmony with the promptings of The Holy Spirit. He must then communicate this positively back to everyone in the group. Clear targets and goals should be established, and thoroughly explained, that will motivate individuals to become enthusiastic about the project. Questions and queries need to aired and dealt with so everyone can see how their contributions will contribute to the overall vision of the group. This will often determine whether people choose to commit to the group or not.

(iii) An Enabling Structure is one where tasks are allocated to people according to their skills and experience and individuals are encouraged to work together in an atmosphere of mutual learning and support. The Christian Leader should establish and clearly define the decision making processes after full and frank discussion with members of the group to ensure that everyone has an equal opportunity to contribute without allowing anyone to either dominate the proceedings or to abdicate from their responsibilities. Everyone should know who to speak to if there is a problem and who to turn to for additional help and support.

(iv) The supportive content of the group is about ensuring that everybody is able to access all the information they may need to perform effectively. The Christian Leader must allow for the development of each person in skill, knowledge and experience with appropriate rewards being provided that highlight the cooperation and achievement of each individual as well as those of the group. Various forms of help and support should be made readily available with clear guidelines of how this can be accessed along with heaps of personal encouragement for each person. Specific help and guidance should be planned in advance whether it is needed or not so that no-one feels isolated or vulnerable.

(v) The provision of high quality Coaching and Mentoring is seen as the final mark of a highly successful group. This will reflect the Christian Leader's ability to identify those people who would benefit most from this kind of help with their personal development and will act as a significant boost for the group as a whole. It will rely also on the leader's ability to bring in the very best people who are able to provide this level of service for his team. This kind of support may sometimes continue even after the objectives of the group have been achieved because of the leader's desire to see people grow into maturity.

This philosophy, like all of the others we have reviewed, requires the very practical involvement of the leader in the day-to-day activities of the group and a very personal level of contact with the individual members of the group. Christian Leadership is no substitute for either of these responsibilities but any leader who chooses to adopt this approach will need the supernatural guidance and direction of The Holy Spirit on a daily basis to be able to perform these tasks effectively.

8. A Sequential Philosophy for Christian Leadership

Sometimes referred to as the Leadership Doughnut

(i) Vision
(ii) Plan
(iii) Reality Test
(iv) Communicate

(v) Resource and Recruit
(vi) Organise and Coordinate
(vii) Support and Motivate
(viii) Guide and Develop

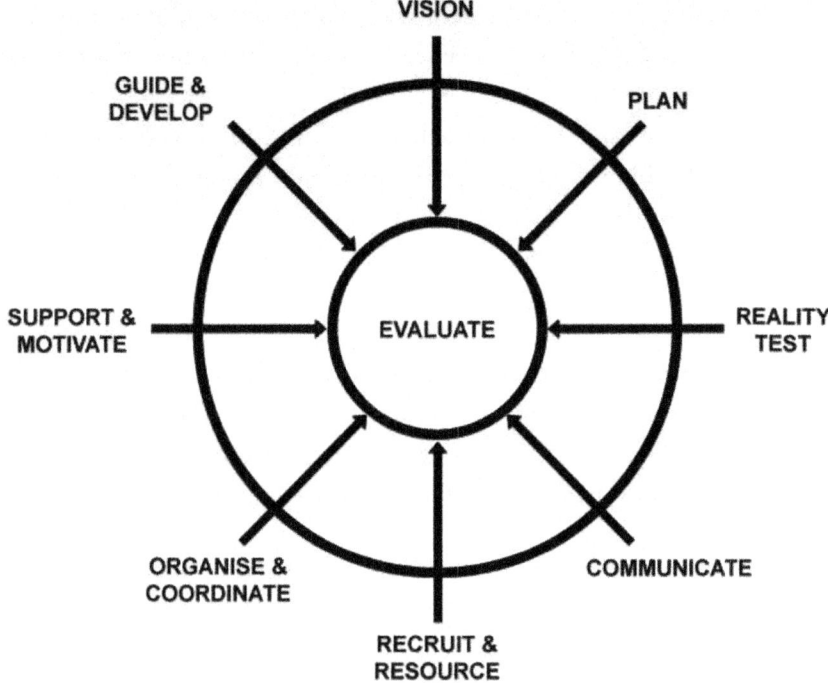

Diagram No8 A Sequential Philosophy
Adapted from Charles Handy's Doughnut Principle (1994)

This approach to leadership involves a constant process of moving from one aspect to another around the circle with the inclusion of a previously agreed system of evaluation. The evaluation could be carried out in a variety of ways but should include the active participation of all the members of the group and be utilised at every stage.

(i)   VISION. The process begins with the establishment of a clear and concise vision for the group which then needs to be prayerfully tested and evaluated before being communicated enthusiastically and comprehensively to the whole group. This should focus on the main objectives of the group but also include elements that will meet the individual needs of people in the group. The Christian Leader should take the initiative here but be very careful not to dominate proceedings.

(ii)   PLAN. The next step is to develop a plan of action by having full discussions with those in the group. This, although time consuming, encourages each person to be involved in the process and to see how they fit into the overall scheme of things. The Christian Leader will require great patience here in order to avoid rushing ahead by dictating his own ideas. The best plans will always include the maximum involvement of the members of the group.

(iii) REALITY TEST. The reality testing part of this approach is intended to enable each member of the group to recognise that the objectives are actually achievable and that they will each receive some significant benefit. The group should realise the importance of the tasks being undertaken and see how these will work together towards achieving the overall objectives. It will be extremely difficult to keep people motivated if the members of the group cannot see how their objectives are going to be achieved.

(iv)   COMMUNICATE. The positive communication of these principles is now essential, not only for the members of the group, but for those who will ultimately benefit from this programme and for those who may be required to back it. Both internal and external support can be generated in this way and the Christian Leader should ensure that no misunderstandings are allowed to exist.

(v)   RESOURCE & RECRUIT. Getting the right people on board now becomes a vital part of this process to ensure that whatever skills or resources may be required to facilitate the project can be accessed when they are needed. The Christian Leader should ensure, as far as possible, that these are all in place to avoid risks of the project stagnating at a later date. This may require additional attention as the project moves ahead and situations change.

(vi)   ORGANISE & COORDINATE. The allocation of the various roles and responsibilities should be based on the skills, talents, and experience of the members of the group so that everyone can see that this process is being handled openly and fairly. People also need to understand how they should relate to others around them and where the boundaries of responsibility lie. The Christian Leader should constantly monitor every area of activity to ensure that harmony and cooperation is maintained at all levels.

(vii) SUPPORT & MOTIVATE. The need to provide on-going support and motivation for all aspects of the work can easily be overlooked with the result that people can begin to feel isolated and lack any acknowledgement for the role they are playing. The Christian Leader should never underestimate the value of maintaining good connections with every member of the group by being able to identify where additional help is needed before it becomes obvious. This should be provided in a completely non-threatening and confidential manner.

(viii) GUIDE & DEVELOP. However successful the project may be (or not), the Christian Leader must not lose sight of his responsibility regarding the on-going development of the individuals in his group. To focus on the objectives of the project to the exclusion of the individuals who are involved is a huge mistake that many leaders make. Consistent attention to the needs and aspirations of the members of the group are essential qualities of Christian Leadership.

Although this is a sequential model, and there is a natural progression around the doughnut, it is not unusual to go back and forth over some elements as the work progresses. However, this can be kept to a minimum by ensuring that an open and comprehensive evaluation process is conducted at every stage.

This style of Christian Leadership is only likely to become the characteristic of someone who is consistently well organised, who possesses great attention for detail, who is a careful, long term planner, and who has a compassionate heart for people. We will discuss these individual characteristics in more detail in Part 4.

In conclusion of this section, there are many more patterns of leadership which we could have mentioned. This is not intended to be an exhaustive list because more are continuing to emerge as time goes by. Whatever system a Christian Leader may choose to adopt, there are two double-principles that are absolutely essential if his work is to be effective;

- Firstly, (a) he will need to have a daily, personal, on-going relationship with God through The Holy Spirit, and (b) he will need to be able to maintain a constant and close working relationship with his followers. Being wholly surrendered to God on a daily basis will enable him to hear His voice and sense His guidance over every issue, plus, having a close relationship to his followers will allow him to make appropriate responses to their needs as the project progresses.
- Secondly, (a) he will need to put an appropriate emphasis on the spiritual development of his individual followers, and (b) he will help to develop this within the framework of the wider objectives of the group. To recognise that every person is a spiritual being who is undergoing a process of transformation by The Holy Spirit, and then to cooperate with this whilst maintaining progress towards the objectives of the group, are qualities that only dedicated Christian Leaders will be able to sustain.

For any leader, the ability to maintain these principles, and constantly hold them in balance, is what will mark out his leadership as being specifically Christian and will make it significantly different from every other pattern or style of leadership.

PART 3

ESSENTIAL WARNINGS FOR
THE CHRISTIAN LEADER

Essential Warnings for the Christian Leader

We come now to consider some serious warnings about certain attitudes to leadership which any person is capable of falling into without realising it, but which cannot be condoned as being acceptable responses for the Christian Leader. It must be emphasised at this point that, similar to the elements of good qualities we all possess, we all have elements of these undesirable qualities also. Therefore, this is not meant to be a 'witch hunt' and is not intended to condemn people who may know no better, but I want to flag up some of the serious deficiencies which can quickly become dominant factors if they are not comprehensively dealt with as soon as they are recognised.

Some of these characteristics are adapted and expanded from the work of the psychologist Jeffrey E. Young who, in 1990, identified a range of negative personality traits as part of his developmental work in Cognitive Therapy. He initially called these 'Lifetraps' and went on to explain how, if allowed to persist, they would limit the way a person would be able to respond to other people and to the world around them. From a leadership point of view these are definitely to be classed as Lifetraps because, if they are allowed to continue unchallenged, they are likely to wreck the potential of even the most talented leader and risk leaving their work in ruins.

I confess that I have fallen into a number of these Lifetraps myself in the past and I know this will have hurt and offended others who were around me at the time. My on-going concern about this is that I may never know the depth of the damage my selfishness caused on those occasions and I am deeply saddened that I am unable to rectify or seek the forgiveness of many of those I have offended. This is part of what motivates me to want to help others avoid falling into similar kinds of negative and destructive behaviours.

Whatever qualities of character a person may possess, the chances are they will have become ingrained as a result of influences and experiences they went through during childhood and early life. Of course, many of these may be very good qualities but we are concerned at this point to identify some of the most negative and destructive ones that must be recognised, challenged and overcome. For Christians it is important to understand that this is not merely a matter of receiving prayer, although that will inevitably help, but it is about changing some of the deep-rooted attitudes and behaviours that have subconsciously become second nature. The good news here is that whatever negative or dysfunctional qualities we may discover about ourselves (including those that may be pointed out to us by other people), there is a way in which we can effectively deal with these. These responses will not generally disappear of their own accord, in fact generally, they will only get worse as time goes by and can rarely be conquered without help.

Therefore, if you suffer in any of these ways, the very best remedy is to immediately consult a competent and qualified Christian Counsellor who, under the guidance of The Holy Spirit, is willing to work with you over a period of time to give you the tools you need to experience victory over these issues. I don't believe there is any issue which cannot be satisfactorily resolved in this way but it will require a high level of honesty and determination for you to accomplish this.

There can be a great deal of similarity between some of the characteristics we will consider here, but also some other very similar qualities may emerge as we explore these. For this reason it is important to be careful before settling on any specific diagnosis and not to be judgemental of anyone else. Whilst we should try to be very critical of ourselves we must remember never to point the finger at other people.

Here are some key character traits that definitely need to be defeated :-

(i)   The Charismatic Leader
(ii)   The Defeatist Leader
(iii)   The Defensive Leader
(iv)   The Dependent Leader
(v)   The Dictatorial Leader
(vi)   The Emotionally Deprived Leader
(vii)   The Fearful Leader
(viii) The Immature Leader
(ix)   The Inhibited Leader

(x)   The Narcissistic Leader
(xi)   The Over-Confident Leader
(xii) The Perfectionist Leader
(xiii) The Self-Sacrificial Leader
(xiv) The Socially Isolated Leader
(xv)   The Undisciplined Leader
(xvi) The Vulnerable Leader

(i) The Charismatic Leader

In Christian circles this is often taken to mean a person who is filled with The Holy Spirit and who demonstrates God's supernatural power in everyday situations. However, non-Christian leaders can also be referred to as 'charismatic' because of the personality and charm they exude. However, we must be aware of the potential dangers that anyone may inadvertently develop and that there are some really negative aspects that can emerge with charismatic leadership.

Charismatic leaders are able to generate great public appeal by their outgoing and energetic personality. Their compelling charm and confident manner creates a desire in people to want to be associated with them but they can develop a need to be indispensible and this will eventually inhibit the development of their followers. Their strong positivity is liable to create blindness to some potentially dangerous situations both for them and their followers because they don't like to be questioned and don't easily admit to making mistakes.

They can exhibit a consistent failure to learn and this can result in them putting down any person who challenges them. Consequently they can become increasingly dictatorial which then tends to makes their followers become increasingly passive. They often develop grand schemes for power and success which can cause them to lose concern for their followers. This, in turn, can lead to an increase in their level of manipulation and/ or deception of others. Finally, their approach is marked by a complete inability to see the need to train and develop people to become their successors.

(ii) The Defeatist Leader

This is a person who is continually struggling with their own failures from the past and who feels completely powerless to overcome these. Their experiences result in a strong sense of inertia and an overwhelmingly negative attitude towards everything around them. This causes them to constantly compare themselves with others and come to the conclusion that they will never be able to make the grade.

They have a pessimistic attitude about everything which prevents them from being willing to move forward. They will tend to find genuine and plausible reasons for this which they will then use to convince their followers. They are completely unwilling to experiment with anything new and have no ability to plan ahead. Their fear of the unknown becomes a dominant factor which results in simply seeking to maintain the status quo.

They will focus strongly on the need to consolidate where they are now and consequently will tend to avoid any opportunities to develop a vision for the future. They are quick to point out potential problems even before they appear and will warn their followers about the dangers of trying to pioneer something new by always assuming the worst.

(iii) The Defensive Leader

A person is liable to exhibit a defensive attitude towards others if they think they are being threatened in some way. This is not an uncommon feeling amongst leaders who may think that someone is becoming too challenging or wants to replace them, but it is actually a sign of a very fragile self-esteem. It is an attitude that undermines relationships because the leader is constantly attempting to justify his actions as a means of reinforcing his superiority.

It is the evidence of someone who has a closed mind and is therefore unwilling to listen to a different point of view. Leaders become inward looking, often secretive, in ways that inhibit natural conversation because they always want to protect their own ideas. This demonstrates a lack of trust, shows a lack of concern for others, and can result in them becoming increasingly withdrawn by choosing to avoid people.

Defensive leaders begin to be dogmatic and argumentative, often fiercely defending their own views by manipulation and impulsive over-reaction. They can be abrasive, critical and judgemental and use this as a way of keeping others at a distance. They are resistant to change by not allowing others to take significant leadership responsibilities or to pioneer new developments in case they prove to be more successful. They can't afford to get involved with the feelings of others and rarely show any emotion of their own which causes them eventually to lose touch with their followers.

(iv) The Dependent Leader

This is a person who simply cannot make decisions on their own and will go to incredible lengths to avoid the responsibility of doing so. Dependent leaders are masters of deflection, preferring always to put the responsibility onto someone else. Such an attitude usually develops as a result of failures from the past and a fear of the ridicule that might be directed towards them if a bad decision is made.

They are 'people-pleasers' who are afraid of falling out with anyone, so their total lack of confidence compels them to try to keep everyone happy. In order to do this they resort to never telling anyone the whole story about anything. They live in a world of half-truths with a desperate need to obtain people's approval. Any information they pass out is filled with 'smoke-and-mirrors' – emphasising work that is going on behind the scenes without giving any specific details – full of platitudes and generalisations.

They continually try to prompt people to respond to them by giving insufficient or limited information about situations and forthcoming events. They are indecisive procrastinators who wait for other people to make decisions and consequently have little original thought but instead try to copy what others are doing. Their lives are filled with anxiety and a dread that people will see through them and become aware of their lack of relevant skills. They are unable to manage any form of conflict, but revert to drawing attention to the difficulties and obstacles they are facing personally.

(v) The Dictatorial Leader

This is someone who is convinced they have the answer to every problem and are the only person who can determine the job or role for everyone else. They are control freaks who dictate all the policies and procedures for the group and demand compliance from everyone. They can be arrogant and their autocratic style leaves no room for innovation or creativity because they see this as a personal threat. They discourage individuality and reject original thinking.

They pay little regard for the feelings of others and frequently have no concern for the issues with which others are struggling. They are highly motivated to achieve their own goals, often at the expense of other people in their group. Their need to take ownership of everything makes them unwilling to consult anyone within their group, even those who may be more experienced. They tend to attract weak workers and cannot create a positive, empowering work environment because they use people to accomplish their own ends (Finzel 2007 p108).

They generally don't understand the benefit of building teams but prefer instead to keep all responsibility to themselves. Consequently they choose to surround themselves with people who won't question their decisions. They can be quick to point out the mistakes of others and to apportion blame, often coming down harshly on the perpetrators. They often have a desire to micro-manage people and this can produce a poor morale which increases the likelihood of people feeling frustrated and wanting to leave the group.

(vi) The Emotionally Deprived Leader

This is a person who is unable to maintain mature relationships because they need constant reassurance from others. They are inward looking and self-protective. They are extremely uncomfortable around people and generally demonstrate a lack of any social skills. Their inability to relate to the feelings of others usually comes from their own experiences of being neglected, abandoned or abused in the past. This can make them suspicious of anyone who wants to show them affection.

They can be extremely sensitive to any form of criticism but are afraid of showing that they cannot cope. This produces high levels of anxiety which can develop into depressive episodes. They are hesitant, insecure and lonely, often choosing to socially isolate themselves. They are prone to change their mind frequently but feel unable to ask anyone for help. They are often seen trying to prove their capabilities and justify their actions. They sometimes have a major difficulty with finishing jobs or tasks.

They are disorganised, indecisive and unsure of themselves yet they often launch into daring and courageous behaviours because of their inability to say 'no'. They can be aggressive, as a self- defence measure, but most often are suffering from inertia, tiredness and guilt. They tend to doubt their own abilities and consequently can doubt God. They are fearful, self-centred and unable to express any empathy towards others.

(vii) The Fearful Leader

This is a nervous person who is filled with trepidation about everything. They are extremely insecure and because they are afraid of showing any weakness they try to appear to be busy all the time. This manifests itself in an over-attentiveness to details which then tends to stifle progress. They struggle with the dilemma of being afraid to get too close to others yet are afraid of being alone and so can become quite clingy.

They lack self confidence and so avoid making decisions in case they are criticised. They are masters of procrastination. They are desperate to please people but continually expect people to take advantage of them which makes them suspicious of everyone. Their negative attitude predisposes them to hate change, preferring instead to vigorously protect what they already know.

They are apprehensive and hesitant and will frequently tolerate inefficiency in others rather than help them deal with it. They find it extremely hard to trust people and are sceptical of anyone who wants to help them. They are afraid to let go of anything and are therefore unable to delegate in case someone else's work doesn't come up to their expectations or, worse still, someone else does a better job than they could do themselves. They have an intense fear losing face (Finzel 2007).

(viii) The Immature Leader

Immaturity is nothing to do with age but is demonstrated by a person who continues to demonstrate childish attitudes and behaviours. They appear unable to take anything seriously and frequently duck their responsibility by making jokes about everything. They often make excuses about their own behaviour and are half-hearted about anything that does not go their own way. They may hide from problems or dismiss them as being unimportant. They are inconsistent and are quick to blame others when mistakes come to light.

They distrust the motives of others and put down people who are close to them. They are unable to effectively coach or mentor others and require people to prove themselves before they are given any responsibility, preferring instead to show favouritism towards their friends. They often rely on gossip and hearsay to form their opinions and will ignore the wisdom of those who may be more experienced.

Their selfish lack of humility often causes them to lose focus on important issues and then become highly defensive of their own opinions. They are not above using intimidation to remain superior and to get their own way. This makes it extremely difficult for them to learn from their mistakes.

(ix) The Inhibited Leader

This a person who is suffering from a psychological weakness which means that they feel controlled by past events and negative experiences. These cause their thinking to be severely restricted because of the fear of a possible repeat. It makes them exceptionally cautious and hesitant about making any decisions. They are very self-conscious, often being shy and withdrawn.

They rarely show any emotion, choosing instead to mask their true feelings. They are nervous, indecisive and tense, but easily embarrassed. They try to carefully control their exposure and prefer to be a 'backroom' person. They will go to great lengths to avoid any form of conflict and are quite unable to deal with it if it occurs.

Their guarded attitude to everything restricts their ability to think freely or creatively. They lack any sense of spontaneity and find it difficult to be really enthusiastic or passionate about anything. They are weak decision makers but make it difficult for others to be actively involved and their reserved lack of authenticity often allows conflict to develop.

(x) The Narcissistic Leader

The characteristics of this person are marked by their constant manipulation and exploitation of others. Their charming attitude belies their underlying need to take advantage of people. They demand recognition and go out of their way to win people over by building up their hopes before dropping them suddenly. They are shameless self-promoters and bullies frequently using lying and misleading strategies to achieve their own ends.

They can be impulsive and unconventional, sometimes throwing tantrums to get their own way, because they are concerned solely with their own image. They appear caring and considerate, frequently exaggerating their achievements in order to get people on their side and to hide their self-centredness. They are arrogant and proud glory seekers.

They are very controlling, believing they alone have the answer to every problem, but they are unpredictable and can break faith in an instant. They never share the whole story about anything and are unable to recognise flaws in their own agenda. Their energy and enthusiasm is totally selfish and it causes people eventually to become demoralised and de-motivated. They are quite unable to express any empathy for others and have no vision and no desire to coach people to be their successors.

(xi) The Over-Confident Leader

This is a person who always needs to be right, about everything, but is motivated solely by their own priorities. They are personal kingdom builders who override the needs and priorities of others. They want to control everything and actually believe that no-one else is able to do what they do. They think they are better than they really are but their excessive self confidence overshadows their lack of ability.

They are frequently a 'one-man-band' type of person who is blind to the qualities of other people. They are controlling, independent and arrogant 'know-it-alls' who make poor leadership role models. They stifle discussion, ignore advice and choose not to allow themselves to be accountable to anyone.

They consider themselves to be better than other people but are prone to make decisions over aspects in which they have little knowledge or experience by railroading things through. They lack any real humility and avoid warnings from those who care about them. Their unrealistic expectations often cause them to fail to honour their commitments. They can hold out promises to people which they have no intention of keeping.

(xii) The Perfectionist Leader

This is a person of unrelenting standards where nothing is ever good enough. They dwell endlessly on mistakes people have made in the past and will constantly find fault with the standards of current work. They are dissatisfied and critical of everything which dramatically increases the levels of stress and anxiety among their workers with the result that people feel devalued and ignored.

They are people who live on the edge, unable to relax and are extremely impatient. They are selfish, inward looking people who lack any empathy for others. This generates a lack of trust for people around them and is often a cause of losing sight of the bigger picture. Their tendency to be picky and have no flexibility comes across as being harshly judgemental which increases the pressure on others and removes any sense of joy in the work.

They are fiercely competitive and won't ask anyone for help. This selfish attitude often causes delays in producing results and this, in turn, can produce feelings of frustration and anger in the workers. People quickly become disillusioned and de-motivated because everything is a battle.

(xiii) The Self Sacrificial Leader

The major difficulty with the self sacrificial leader is their lack of attention to personal matters. They are so committed to do everything they can for the benefit of others that they neglect themselves and their own family. Their personal life is a mess with bills unpaid, jobs not completed and promises broken. They are not good leadership role models.

They are driven by the need to keep up appearances which means they must be seen to be doing all that is expected of them, and more. They are caught up with every minor distraction and every request for help. They have no ability to say 'no'. They put unnecessary pressure on themselves, are always in a hurry over everything, often arriving late for meetings and can easily lose sight of the overall objectives of the group.

They are consumed by guilt and the fear that someone will expose their weaknesses and failings. Outwardly they put on a brave face but inwardly they are permanently stressed, often near to breaking point. They are a car crash waiting to happen and are incapable of keeping all their plates spinning yet are invariably willing to take on even more. They have no time to plan, find it hard to involve other people, and refuse to make themselves accountable to anyone.

(xiv) The Socially Isolated Leader

This is a person who is extremely self conscious and chooses to cut themselves off from others. They consider themselves to be not good enough in a variety of ways which predisposes them to be unwilling to meet people. They feel inferior and without status which causes them to believe that they really don't belong, consequently their involvement in activities and their participation in events is often minimal.

Their poor relationship skills demonstrate the lack of an appropriate support group which increases their feelings of isolation. They are socially inept, often experiencing poor health, and can be prone to bouts of anxiety and depression. They believe they are unattractive and flawed in character and their lack of social interaction substantially increases their personal levels of stress. They constantly live in fear of things going wrong or of some tragedy catching them unawares and will frequently hide from, and be unavailable to people.

(xv) The Undisciplined Leader

This is a person who has a minimum amount of self control and is therefore easily distracted or drawn away at tangents. They are poor timekeepers, unreliable, inconsistent, and lack clear leadership principles. Their lack of self awareness allows them to drift into a casual attitude about personal levels of commitment. They frequently let people down but seem to have no undue concern about this. They lack the ability to plan ahead and consequently develop poor routines and have little structure for their work.

Their outward charm often hides the fact that they are complacent, erratic and sometimes lazy. They tend to accept low standards by overlooking important details. They waste time on trivialities and lose focus on the bigger issues. They establish poor boundaries and have a limited respect for authority. Their spontaneity makes them liable to addictive behaviour and their lack of skills predisposes them to tolerate negative attitudes and conversations within the group.

(xvi) The Vulnerable Leader

This is someone who believes they are continually on the verge of some catastrophic event and consequently they feel permanently exposed to harm or attack. They have a negative view of everything and constantly suffer from high levels of stress and anxiety. Their expectation that problems are about to occur leads them to take excessive and unnecessary precautions for their own self protection. They become excessively needy, constantly seeking assurance and protection from others.

They may take on a weak defenceless attitude by attempting to hide from difficulties without realising this actually makes them more susceptible to challenges and problems. Their passivity demonstrates little resistance and they portray themselves as frail and gullible. They become totally inward looking people who are determined to constantly warn others about all the difficulties they are facing, on a daily basis.

In conclusion of this section, it must be said that characteristics such as these are only likely to become dominant in people who are extremely self-centred to the degree that the whole focus of their lives revolves around their own desire to achieve their own objectives. This can happen to such an extent that they will then only endorse those things that appear to be of benefit to others if there is some personal gain to be achieved. Whilst their drive and enthusiasm is often to be admired, their misplaced loyalty will let them, and their followers, down every time.

In this context, we must not be fooled by outward appearances. These people will frequently be those who get things done and, in the process, often attract a large following, but there will be a trail of disappointed and disillusioned people left in their wake. There is also likely to be a large number of issues that are not being adequately addressed or are being swept under the carpet and this is likely to produce a high turnover of followers.

PART 4

ESSENTIAL QUALITIES FOR
THE CHRISTIAN LEADER

Essential Qualities for the Christian Leader

We come now to consider the qualities of excellence to which all leaders should aspire, but for the Christian Leader, these should be considered absolutely essential if a strong witness is to be maintained. Once again, there are many attributes that could be included here and many variations of the ones which do appear here. This is not an exhaustive list but it is intended to draw attention to some of the most important qualities every Christian Leader should aim to develop. Everybody has the potential for all of these qualities but they don't come to fruition automatically. The challenge therefore is that only those who choose to work at them will be able to demonstrate them effectively. For this to be most successful it will require the Christian Leader to have a resolute faith in the supernatural sovereignty of Almighty God and to be completely open in heart and mind to listen, to hear, to understand what He is saying and to be willing to be stretched beyond their own ability.

1. Visionary Praying & Planning

(i)   Perceiving the Dilemmas
(ii)   Pinpointing the Destinations
(iii)   Plotting the Directions
(iv)   Pre-empting the Difficulties
(v)   Pioneering the Developments

"Where there is no vision (or revelation), the people cast off restraint", (or do whatever they want) Proverbs 29 v18.

For the Christian Leader there can be no more important activity than that of praying. However, this is not just about asking God to bless the decisions that have already been made, but it is a continuous process of seeking God's guidance and instruction before anything is attempted and then continuing to pray on through every subsequent step of the journey. It begins with the need to develop a clear understanding of what the challenges are and how God wants them to be tackled.

This kind of visionary praying and planning is only possible once an identifiable objective has been established and as part of a continuously close personal relationship with The Lord. This should, therefore, become an absolute priority for the Christian Leader. It is not to do with telling God what the problem is, nor describing to Him how you perceive it, but it is having the ability to clearly hear and understand what He is saying about the situation. Praying with vision requires a genuine on-going passion to receive directly from The Lord what the details of His plans and purposes are.

(i) Perceiving the Dilemmas

When Nehemiah heard from his brother about the terrible state of the city of Jerusalem he committed himself to fasting and prayer for four months before taking any action whatsoever (Nehemiah 1 v 4 and 2 v 1). Even then, when the king asked him what he wanted, he immediately shot up an arrow prayer before giving him a list of the things God told him he would need (Nehemiah 2 v 7-8). During his times of prayer and fasting God had downloaded to Nehemiah a plan of action and given him a detailed description of some of the materials that would be required if he was going to undertake the job.

Before Nehemiah agreed to take on the work, it was important that he was under no illusions about what was involved, and he needed to be aware of some of the obstacles he would be likely to face. Through his times of prayer, I believe God was able to give Nehemiah a vision of what he was about to undertake and this prompted him to ask his king for a number of specific things.

If we don't understand something of the challenges we are about to face, and have some idea about how God is asking us to tackle these, we will be working blindly and will be unable to provide constructive leadership for others. God always sees a bigger picture than we do and He always has a master plan that often exceeds our ability to comprehend (Ephesians 2 v 20). This means that we will never know the full extent of the problems before we start, but we do need to know that we are following

God's plans and purposes rather than our own and that we have made the choice to draw at all times on the resources He makes available to us.

(ii) Pinpointing the Destinations

The next vital aspect of our praying and planning is to obtain a clear understanding of what our objectives are to be because every future step in our work of leadership hinges on this. Without it we could be labouring in vain, going round in circles, or failing to make progress, all of which will create frustration among our followers, negate our leadership position, and fail to achieve the desired outcomes. Now I am aware that sometimes The Lord will ask us to step out in faith without telling us where He is taking us, but whenever He is asking us to lead others I believe He will always give us a specific destination to aim for. It seems that in leadership situations He is more likely to give us a specific destination without telling us how He wants us to get there.

Leaders who are vague about their destination will be hesitant and uncertain in their leadership. If we are in any doubt about our destination, we should be persistent in asking The Lord to show us the objective to which He is calling us. Jesus had no hesitation in following exactly what The Father was telling Him because He knew His destination (John 13 v 3). This is borne out by what Jesus said to His disciples (John 4 v 34) and in His final prayer in the garden of Gethsemane (John 17 v 4).

> **Our ability to handle the problems we encounter in leadership will be in direct proportion to the certainty we have that we are doing God's Will.**

Leadership is always going somewhere and is never static, but people will only be motivated to follow when we can give them a clear sense of the destination that is linked to what God has already placed within them. If we try to promote a destination that is of our own making, people will quickly lose interest, so we must pray with vision and expectancy. That means we must be willing for The Lord to show us things that are beyond our ability to see in the physical dimension and to recognise that He will often have more than one objective in mind for us.

God's ultimate destination for all of us is a spiritual one therefore every task or project we undertake in Christian Leadership will also have a spiritual purpose that will be of benefit to every person who is involved. We must never lose sight of this. We should also appreciate that it is perfectly OK to ask The Lord to give us more detail when we are unsure about anything. It is a common failing in all aspects of leadership to rush off 'half-cocked' into planning an activity that is based on only half the information we need. This is sometimes God's way of testing whether we are really listening to Him.

Such misplaced enthusiasm can get us into all kinds of trouble if we don't have persistence in our praying but instead choose to put our own interpretation onto what we are hearing. This becomes much more likely when we believe we already possess the skill and ability to face the challenge before us. So whether we feel strong or weak, it should make no difference to our desire to have a clear picture from The Lord about the destinations He wants us to aim for before we set about making any detailed plans.

(iii) Plotting the Directions

This aspect of leadership can only begin once a clear and specific destination is obtained. It is the process of putting enough stepping stones in the river that will enable us to get to the other side. This will generally involve breaking down the journey into its smallest constituent parts in order to ensure that every person in the group can play their part and that each person will still be there at the completion. There will often be quicker and easier ways of achieving an objective, but the role of the Christian Leader is not about speed or personal accomplishment, it is about encouraging every person to grow and mature as they use their own gifts and abilities for the common good.

In the sport of Orienteering, it is only possible to work out which is likely to be the best route to the next check-point when the location of it has been clearly identified. Similarly in leadership, once the destination has been prayerfully identified the overall direction of the group can be established and the detailed planning can begin. This then becomes the next emphasis for prayer, but it also needs to be done in close collaboration with all the members of the group because it is vital for each person to see that their individual objectives are also being taken into consideration.

The real skill of Christian Leadership is to encourage every person to use their unique mixture of gifts, skills, talents and abilities in cooperation with one another so that their own goals as well as those of the group can be achieved.

There is no instant solution here because it will need to involve a regular connection with each of the members of the group along with much careful and prayerful thought, discussion and planning together. When the leader is able to do this effectively he will find that it raises the sense of expectation within the group and this, in turn, will increase the productivity and progress towards the overall vision. When Moses set in motion the plans God had given him for the building of the Tabernacle he involved as many skilled people as he could. Even those who weren't skilled were able to get involved by learning and working alongside others who were already experienced (1 Kings 35 v 35 – 36 v 1). This is a great example of Christian Leadership.

(iv) Pre-empting the Difficulties

It is most important for the Christian Leader to remain positive at all times, but that does not mean that he should be unaware or ill-prepared for possible difficulties that may be encountered along the way. In fact, to demonstrate a readiness to face these, and not be taken by surprise, will build increased confidence in the rest of the group. The Christian Leader must accept his challenges with his eyes wide open at all times and never adopt a blinkered approach to his work.

As mentioned earlier, it will never be possible to know in advance all the difficulties that might be encountered in any challenge, which is why it is so important to keep hearing from The Lord on a regular basis. This is what enables God to prompt and guide the Christian Leader into different aspects of personal and corporate preparation because this can often include things which initially appear to be unimportant or even unconnected but which may become really significant at a later date.

When Joseph had received, and delivered, his interpretation of Pharaoh's dreams (Genesis Ch. 41), he initiated a programme of building and harvesting and storing food supplies that would enable the whole country to survive the intense famine that was to come seven years later. Some may refer to this kind of thing as 'a word of knowledge' or 'a word of prophecy' but however it is perceived, the fact is that God speaks to us and, because He knows the end even from the beginning, He wants us to be prepared for all the difficulties that lie ahead.

There is a sense in which every single situation we face, whether good, bad or indifferent, is part of the way God prepares us for something He may bring across our path further down the line. Such things could crop up very soon afterwards or be a long way off but the Christian Leader should constantly try to instil this principle into his followers both by his teaching and by his example. The role of visionary praying and planning should not the sole prerogative of the leader, although it is essential that he should take the lead in this, but he should make regular efforts to involve every person in the group in the exercise.

(v) Pioneering the Developments

A vital, and frequently overlooked, aspect of visionary praying and planning is having the courage to begin to pioneer new things for God that are in accordance with what He is saying. Too often people will choose to hear everything through what they have known from the past or what they feel they have the ability to achieve rather than to perceive opportunities to break new ground. They may be concerned lest they forget some of the lessons they have learned from the past or simply prefer the security of what they already know. Either way, they can show a lack of enthusiasm to press forward.

Pioneers are people who know how to GO, how to take other people with them, and how to encourage them to do something similar.

Christian Leadership will nearly always involve being a pioneer and this is concerned with Praying, Planning and Progressing. If any one of these elements is missing, the pioneering process will stagnate, the leader will lose credibility, projects will fail, and followers will become disillusioned. A friend once told me that a pioneer should be someone who is:

Progressive,
Innovative,
Overcomer,
Never says Never,
Energetic,
Enterprising, and
Radical.

In the apostle Paul's letter to the Philippian church he stressed the importance of his ability to put behind him any successes from his past in order to be able to focus clearly on the tasks ahead and then to press into those whilst keeping his eyes firmly on his goal (Philippians 3 v 13-14). Walking hand in hand and communicating with The Lord throughout every day is realistically the only way to ensure this is possible. In this way, the Christian Leader will never be fazed by any obstacles or difficulties but will be able to rise to the challenge in the strength The Lord provides.

2. Healthy & Wholesome Living

(i)   Managing your Family
(ii)   Managing your Finance
(iii)   Managing your Fitness

The personal standards which are demonstrated by the Christian Leader are frequently those that will filter down into every area of the work and subconsciously begin to be copied by other members of the group. Whilst this can often be of great comfort and encouragement to the leader, he may not be able to see that his own weaknesses and failings are also likely to be copied in this way.

(i) Managing your Family

In his letter to Timothy, the apostle Paul stressed the necessity for anyone who may be seeking a position of responsibility in the church to be a person who is able to manage his family well (1 Timothy 3 v 4-5). This principle is equally relevant for the Christian Leader in any position within any organisation. So often in Christian circles, well meaning and enthusiastic leaders are neglecting their families because of the pressures of the job they are undertaking. When this happens, however spiritual their role may be, it is likely that they have been blinded into believing they are demonstrating a greater level of commitment to The Lord.

Many Christian leaders fail to recognise that by far their most significant responsibility is to manage their family well. As a useful guide, the amount of quality time spent with spouse and children, which should never be underestimated as a substantial investment in the future and a powerful advertisement for the Kingdom of God, should at least be equal to the amount of time being devoted to the work. So many children (and followers) have turned their back on Christian values because of the way leaders have failed to manage their families.

Right through The Bible we see the predominant significance of the family relationship, and this is portrayed most powerfully by the way Father, Son and Holy Spirit work together and the way it is modelled by how God continually relates to and cares for us, His children.

(ii) Managing your Finance

Although all forms of leadership are primarily about working with people, the way in which the Christian Leader manages his finances speaks a great deal about his sense of priorities. Whilst it is clearly not appropriate for any leader to broadcast all the details of where he spends his money, never-the-less his attitudes towards money (and possessions) will quickly become obvious to his followers. The Christian Leader's example of care and attention to detail in this respect, his attitude towards giving into the work of the Kingdom, his respect of the situation in which others find themselves, and his ability to live within his means, will convey important messages to his followers.

There may well be occasions when the Christian Leader will be called upon to speak about money, perhaps by inviting people to contribute or to sponsor the work in some way. At times like this, his integrity concerning matters of finance will come to the fore and the way in which such finances are handled will become a significant issue. People who give voluntary donations to any organisation really have a right to know how their money is going to be used and be able to see that it is correctly managed by people who are appropriately held accountable.

(iii) Managing your Fitness

This is an area which is frequently and easily overlooked by many active and enthusiastic leaders. Carving out time from a busy work schedule to spend on issues of personal fitness can often be seen as time being stolen from the work to which we have been called. Yet we are reminded in The Bible that we are to treat our bodies as temples of The Holy Spirit (1 Corinthians 6 v 19), so we must make this a priority and give it a specific allocation of our time.

The tasks of managing fitness do not only relate to our levels of physical fitness, but to all aspects of our health and suitability for the work to which we have been appointed. Therefore we must also give due attention to our diet, to our habits, to our relationships, to our activities and interests, as well as to our spiritual condition. All of these can interfere with our readiness to perform the job required of us, and any of these can develop into hindrances and/or major stumbling blocks if we allow inappropriate elements to creep in or let them get out of control.

Christian Leadership in voluntary organisations, charities and churches will often necessitate the leader planning his weekly programme in much more detail to ensure that he can maintain a balance in his schedule and avoid becoming overtired. It can be mentally stimulating to have additional interests outside the work role, but leaders must be careful to ensure these don't become more important than family and work commitments (see appendix E). These matters of personal discipline are so important that they not only help us to be properly mentally and physically prepared for the work, but give us the very best opportunity of consistently performing at the highest level.

3. Active & Perceptive Listening

(i)   Controlling your Readiness
(ii)   Contemplating your Resources
(iii)   Concentrating your Responses
(iv)   Coordinating your Relationships

To understand this quality we must first of all appreciate the difference between active listening and passive listening. Active listening requires us to be involved, or engaged, in the process whereas passive listening requires no response from us at all. Active listening means that we remain focused and attentive the whole time with a sense of expectancy and anticipation yet not pre-empting what is being said to us. Passive listening merely requires us to be hearing what is going on without taking it in. This is similar to the way we might allow the sound of music to waft over us, or accept the murmur of many conversations in a restaurant.

The development of active listening skills is an essential requirement for someone to become an effective Christian Leader because there is a direct comparison between a person's willingness to listen to God and the way they are willing to listen to other leaders, to their followers, and to other people. The way they listen to any one of these is a sure indication of the way they are likely to listen to each of the others. Therefore, if a leader allows a passive listening attitude to develop in any one aspect of his work this will begin to rub off onto each of the other areas also and will demonstrate a lack of interest or willingness to appreciate and understand what is being said to him.

The ability to use active listening skills is inherent in all of us but we rarely practice this or know how to use it constructively. The following skills are generally taught to trainee counsellors because they are essential tools which help to convey a genuine interest in what is being said and play a vital part in building and developing the relationship. They are:

Attending – demonstrating concentration physically and mentally
Reflecting – using minimal encouragers and key words you heard
Paraphrasing – repeating in your own words what has been said
Mirroring – maintaining receptive body language

Clarifying – checking that you have heard correctly
Focusing – keeping attention on the main topic
Summarising – summing up to demonstrate understanding
Empathising – experiencing something of the other's perspective

Without knowing how to use these tools the leader will constantly struggle to maintain a healthy productive relationship with his followers, or with any other important people, and this will be reflected in his ability (or inability) to hear God.

(i) Controlling your Readiness

This doesn't come easily so it will require a serious amount of time and commitment to become a person who is in a constant state of readiness to listen to others. We all think we are good at listening, but if you want to check how good you are, just ask a few people who know you really well. Most will probably say "You're OK", but for the Christian Leader that is just not good enough. Active listening requires practice and this begins with the development of a right attitude and by making a conscious choice to be better at being ready to listen.

The fact about this is that if we don't actually make the effort to develop and train ourselves to be prepared and ready to listen, we will automatically fall into the category of those who think they are listening but are, in reality, barely hearing. Life often teaches us how to appear to be listening without actually paying any attention to what is being said to us. Preparing to listen involves learning how to clear our minds and quieten our thoughts in order to give the maximum amount of our attention to what someone else is saying to us.

This ability is a clear indication of a person who is growing in maturity because it can only be learned with patience over a period of time. We can test ourselves in this respect by noticing the way we respond when people who are closest to us give us feedback on our various activities. If we immediately jump to our own defence by trying to justify our actions, we are not truly listening. We must learn to take on board what people are saying even when we disagree with their comments. We can then continue to develop our skill as we set aside a specific time every day to listen to

God by choosing a time when we are likely to have the least amount of interruptions. As this grows into a habit, we will discover our ability to pay attention to other people begins to rapidly improve.

We all have the ability to make ourselves ready to listen but, if we fail to do this, we will automatically fall into the trap of assuming we know what the other person is about to say. You must have come across a situation where two people are having a discussion and one of them is intent on finishing the sentences of the other, sometimes getting it right and sometimes getting it wrong. It shows a level of impatience on the part of the listener and a lack of appreciation for the importance of what is being said, but most significantly, it is simply rude.

(ii) Contemplating your Resources

This is an aspect of self reflection which will enable us to specifically identify our strengths and weaknesses in the area of listening. As has already been mentioned, the way we choose to listen to God is likely to be the same pattern we adopt when listening to others. This is what makes it important for us as Christian Leaders to review from time to time our patterns of listening and to make ourselves aware of any bad habits we may be falling into.

We all find it easier to listen to some people and much more difficult to listen to others. Therefore we should identify the people we find hardest to listen to and analyse why that should be the case. Is it the way they speak, the language they use, the topics they cover, or the occasions they choose? Is it our availability, our workload, our levels of patience, or the focus of our attention? As we consider these questions we must also consider what message this conveys to our followers.

The level of our success as a Christian Leader is likely to be in direct proportion to our willingness to pay attention to and listen to our followers. Of course, there is never enough time to do everything we would like to do, nor to spend as much time as we would like on certain activities, so we must review what is within our remit to be changed. Part of this will involve checking out how much we are doing in our own strength, how much we are relying on the work of others, and how much we are drawing on the resources God provides.

Frequently the first sign of stress or burnout in a leader is when they are unable to listen effectively. When leaders don't have time to listen to their followers they are simply too busy and need to urgently consider making some changes to their schedule. This also raises questions about their motivation and their goals and ambitions. We all have the ability to get so caught up with our own objectives that we lose sight of the reason we are in a position of leadership and what the calling is that God has placed on our lives. We must never allow these issues to get out of perspective.

(iii) Concentrating your Responses

Every leader should conduct a regular self review of their working practices in order to be aware of the way they are responding to the situations and the people around them. Active and perceptive listening always goes beyond simply what people are saying, so the Christian Leader will want, on every occasion, to be able to pick up on the messages behind the spoken words. In other words, to also understand what is NOT being said. We must constantly ask ourselves "Am I able to hear the person's heart and to sense what they are feeling rather than just hear their voice, and how am I responding to this awareness?"

This may involve learning some new skills and developing different ways of reacting to people so as to portray a more caring and compassionate style of leadership. It will, nearly always, be more time consuming and require a greater level of commitment and involvement in the affairs of others but then, that is what makes Christian Leadership different from all the other approaches. When Jesus called a team together to begin His work on earth He committed Himself to spend practically every waking moment with them for a period of three years, yet He never sacrificed any of His daily commitment to spend time with His Father.

(iv) Coordinating your Relationships

Another important part of active and perceptive listening is the need to coordinate the relationships we have with the people around us so they don't interfere with, but actually enhance, our ability to listen. One of the most amazing things about Jesus is that He never neglected His relationship with His team, He never turned anyone away (except those who wanted to undermine His work), He never missed spending time with His Father and, because of this, He never lost sight of His overall mission.

The Christian Leader must take responsibility to carefully coordinate his relationship with others around him so that everyone is clear about where they fit into the wider scheme of things. Failure to do this will often result in people being offended by misunderstanding their position and not fully grasping the significance of the whole work. They are then more likely to become a distraction by demanding more time and attention which can immediately place an unnecessary burden on the leader.

It is a common mistake for leaders to not give enough attention to this matter because it seems a waste of their time, but failure to do this effectively will serve to increase misunderstandings and store up difficulties which may have to be tackled later. It is perfectly OK to have a closer relationship with some people on your team than you do with others, provided this does not exclude or marginalise anyone else. However, this needs to be carefully explained to everyone so that struggles for recognition and status can be avoided. The active and perceptive listening skills of the leader are an important pre-requisite for this.

4. Clear & Consistent Communicating

    (i)   Connecting the Inclinations of People
    (ii)   Clarifying the Intentions of People
    (iii) Coaching the Involvement of People

One of the most common reasons for all kinds of organisations and relationships to fail is the lack, or the breakdown, of clear and consistent communication. We can see it in industry, in commerce, in education, in business and in marriage. When people don't know what is happening or what is being planned they can quickly lose interest and allow their commitment to wane. We all have an inherent need to be valued, recognised and involved in whatever we choose to commit ourselves to. Whenever this is not forthcoming we have a natural tendency to begin to look elsewhere.

This is such an important principle that, in spite of what most people might believe, even God chooses to keep His people informed (Amos 3 v 7, Revelation 10 v 7). In fact, although He continues to speak and guide people individually, anyone can read and study His whole strategy which is set out for us in the pages of The Bible. Our God is a God of revelation whose whole philosophy is to bring about His purposes by working in and through the people He created.

(i) Connecting the Inclinations of People

In order to develop the work of any group, the Christian Leader must first be able to identify what motivates his followers, that is, what constitutes their personal passions and desires. As he makes a connection here he will be able to work to incorporate these into the overall plan for the group so that every person has the opportunity to be actively involved in the programme. This will enable him to take people with him as they tackle the tasks ahead of them because, unless this happens, he will not be able to lead the group effectively.

Without this connection, he will spend a large amount of time and energy trying to persuade his followers to commit to his plan. Effective communication is always a two-way activity which is started by the leader getting onto the same wave-length as his followers. You see, it is impossible to motivate anyone from the outside. Motivation is an internal quality, so to motivate a person we need to get in touch with what is already inside them. Anything other than this will result in the need for increasing amounts of persuasion and this, if unsuccessful, will often result in attempts at manipulation.

On one occasion when I was working as part of a sales team our sales director wanted to motivate us to increase our sales figures. He had set each one of us a challenging new target and then, to motivate us, he offered a reward. He announced "For every person who reaches their target within the prescribed period of time the company will give you and your family an all-expenses-paid week in Majorca". It all sounded great to the person on my right who was highly motivated and said "That's fantastic, I've always wanted to go to Majorca". However the person on my left was not in the least bit motivated because he said "That's a complete waste of time for me because my son owns an apartment in Majorca and I spend 4 weeks there every year"

If these two people had been working together on the same project their differences in motivation levels could have created some strong disagreements. The Christian Leader has a responsibility to identify and then connect with the internal interests and desires of his followers to enable the group to pull together to reach their objectives. When Joshua was leading the Children of Israel into the promised land where each of the twelve tribes had been given their own area of land to inhabit, he was able to get them to see how they needed to fight together to take possession of the whole land before any of them could settle in their own allocated spot (Joshua 1 v 12-15).

Making the connection between the internal desires of individuals within the group, and then communicating this to the group as a whole, can become a powerful factor in blending the efforts of the group into a harmonious and cohesive team. Until this happens, the members of the group are likely to remain a disparate group of individuals who are not able to work effectively as a team.

(ii) Clarifying the Intentions of People

Having established what the internal motivations are of the people in his group, the Christian Leader should now turn his attention to discovering what the members are actually willing and/or able to commit to doing. Since this is so often very different from what they say they would like to do, the leader needs to conduct a reality check with each individual. Many leaders have launched into projects believing their followers are totally committed to the tasks ahead only to discover that their members are already over-committed in other areas of their lives and are simply unable to devote the amount of time that might otherwise be expected of them.

This requires the leader to 'get a feel' for what each person is willing, or able, to contribute to the project and the group rather than simply hearing what they may be saying. Someone once said "The way to hell is paved with good intentions" and although this may sound a bit harsh, leaders can only work with whatever people are actually prepared to do, not what they say.

This should be an important encouragement and discovery phase for both leader and followers as they seek to identify the capability and availability of each person in the group in relation to how their goals and objectives might complement one another.

It requires a time of testing to see whether people are ready to match what they are saying with their preparedness to be involved. Whilst people should be encouraged to have big dreams, their involvement should be limited to taking small steps initially to ensure they are not over-committing themselves in the early stages. This also helps to ensure that their individual goals present no conflict either with the goals of others in the group or with the goals of the project as a whole. This can also be a way of helping people develop their gifts and skills by giving them a safe environment in which to experiment and grow whilst being actively supported.

The more timid and reserved members of the group may need lots of encouragement at this point and, where possible, it can help for them to be partnered to work alongside and with the more confident, capable members. Sensitive leadership is required for this to work effectively but if it is done well it will develop a strong sense of belonging and harmony within the group. It is a mistake to leave people to their own devices or to expect them to work things out for themselves. This will tend to allow disagreements to flourish and leaves room for people to compete for personal recognition.

In the Christian faith, as in life generally, many people can be filled with good intentions yet be unable to translate these into action because they are unwilling or unable to allocate the time to make important changes in their schedule. Frequently people know what The Bible says and may be familiar with its stories but if they don't apply the principles in their life they will never experience the blessings or the benefits that are promised there.

(iii) Coaching the Involvement of People

When the project is underway and people are getting on with their tasks it is a great temptation for the leader to either begin to sit back or to start to become interested in something else. However in Christian

Leadership, the job of the leader continues to be significant. He should be actively involved with each member of the group so that, as the project progresses, he can work with them to help them meet their own objectives. His desire should be to see the people in his group maturing, learning new skills and taking more responsibility as the whole project moves forward.

The principle of Coaching is about helping people improve their skills, overcome obstacles, remain focused, and get to where they want to be (Peck 2014), and at the same time ensuring the work of the group doesn't lose momentum. The role of a competent Coach is often overlooked in Christian circles and consequently lots of opportunities for the continuing growth and development of individuals is lost to the organisation.

This is the stage where people at all levels of their development can be encouraged to break new ground by stepping into a greater level of commitment or to improve their expertise in some way. If the leader has built a strong rapport with his team, most of them will value his input to refine a process that is already happening or to address something that could improve their performance. This kind of trusting relationship has an empowering effect on the whole team and can be an important pre-requisite for the group to move on to their next assignment. It is also a way in which the leader should be modelling what he wants his followers to be doing with regard to the way they encourage and help to develop other people in the group.

5. Sensitive & Systematic Empowering

(i)   Equipping People
(ii) Enabling People
(iii) Employing People

One of the most important qualities of a Christian Leader is the belief that they should be working to put themselves out of a job. Regardless of the position a leader holds, he should be constantly bringing on other people with a view to one of them replacing him at some point so the organisation will be able to move forward into areas that are currently beyond him. However dynamic and revolutionary a leader may be, without a firm commitment to this belief he will eventually become the cork in the bottle, or the one who causes some aspect of the organisation to stagnate.

This principle doesn't relate only to the role of the leader, but it is applicable to every role and every person in the group. The Christian Leader will need to work hard to develop and foster this understanding amongst everyone so that eventually it becomes the commonly accepted practice. In this way each person will then be developing their own skills whilst at the same time helping others to grow and mature. The strong sense of bonding that can be produced in this way between the members of the group can become such a tangible asset that it can transform mundane jobs into opportunities for joyful fellowship.

(i) Equipping People

Every leadership position automatically contains a level of responsibility to be equipping and training others. This will inevitably require a conscious effort on the part of the leader to provide appropriate amounts of teaching and training, especially to those who are showing the potential for leadership, but unfortunately this is frequently overlooked. When the apostle Paul wrote his second letter to Timothy he stressed the importance of him entrusting his message to reliable people who would be able to continue to develop the work (2 Timothy 2 v 2). This is sometimes known as the 222 principle and it should be seen as a vital part of every leader's responsibility.

Of course, it is also the responsibility of every individual to diligently seek to improve themselves, but that doesn't absolve leaders from this necessary task. When Paul wrote to the church in Ephesus he made it clear that even those who are appointed to the roles of Apostle, Prophet, Evangelist, Pastor and Teacher should not be doing all the work themselves but should take on the specific responsibility to be equipping and preparing others to do the work (Ephesians 4 v 12). This is the Biblical pattern for building up churches and it is the way to ensure that every person has a role to play (Ephesians 4 v 16).

This Biblical pattern should be implemented in every company or organisation to create a desire to develop individuals at the same time as taking the work forward. Many of the companies, businesses and organisations that remain successful over a period of time do so because they employ a similar system that consistently seeks to identify, train and develop the next generation of their leaders.

(ii) Enabling People

Whilst furnishing people with appropriate teaching and training may go some way towards meeting their practical needs, if they are to be enabled to operate in their new-found skills and understandings, this will also require the development of a psychological element. It is not unusual for people to lack the confidence to use their skills within a group, where they may be around others who are more talented and more experienced, so the Christian Leader must take the initiative to make space for people to grow in this way and it may involve taking people under his wing and supporting them through this learning process.

When the apostle Paul addressed the church in Rome regarding using their gifts, he explained that it is the collective responsibility of the church to create the space to let people use their gifts (Romans 12 v 6-8). However, those who are occupying positions of leadership must take the lead in this respect otherwise it will never happen. This can often be best achieved by bringing people alongside those in the group who are already more accomplished and who can provide some guidance and encouragement rather than just expecting people to find their own way to put their gifts to use.

We all have responsibility to exercise the gifts we have been given (Matthew 15 v 14-30), but many people will shy away from doing so in case they are criticised for trying to push themselves forward. Therefore, creating an atmosphere in which everyone is encouraged to use their gifts without the fear of making a mistake or of being ridiculed will always be contingent upon the attitude of the leader. When this is modelled by the leader, and he creates the expectation for everyone in the group, people will see that they can learn from every situation even while they are gaining experience themselves because it is a safe controlled environment.

(iii) Employing People

Many people in leadership positions struggle with the concept of actually employing the gifts that other people possess. It means they must begin using members of their group to perform tasks they would normally be doing themselves and which they are perfectly capable of doing themselves. This can generate all sorts of fears for the leader about his image to the outside world, about his standing within the group, and about whether this would jeopardise the project in any way by tolerating a lowering of standards or by accepting an approach which may be different to their own.

The chances are that leaders are only likely to introduce this principle when they have comprehensively followed the previous two principles in this section because it will involve them stepping back, taking their hands off, and resisting the temptation to micro-manage or continuing to control what is going on. It will require a high level of trust to be exercised on the part of both the leader and the team members, and everyone involved will need a clear and specific understanding of the objectives for doing this so any misunderstandings or workings at cross purposes can be avoided.

The maintenance of good lines of communication is an essential ingredient at this point so the leader can keep in touch with progress on all fronts without putting any pressure on the workers. He must resist the need to continually look over the shoulder of his workers yet ensure they know this is not a sign of a lack of interest. The leader's on-going encouragement and support should be evident without being obvious and he should always seek to be available to be consulted whenever the need may arise.

This should be one of the most rewarding aspects of leadership – to see your protégés growing in confidence and maturity by taking responsibility for aspects of the group tasks that will also aid their personal development and growth. This really sums up the role of the Christian Leader and should be a clearly stated objective for every leadership position. There is no greater reward than to watch the people you have trained and nurtured begin to break new ground and take others under their wing in the same way you have done.

The styles and approaches you are modelling in practice are likely to be those you see being repeated by the members of your team. So before you are tempted to criticize any of your team, it is good practice to do a thorough examination of your own actions.

6. Regular & Constant Reproducing

(of more leaders not more followers)

(i)   Recognising Leadership Traits
(ii)   Rehearsing Leadership Talents
(iii) Releasing Leadership Transformers

We now move on to consider the overall process of fulfilling the objectives of the group - which must include the specific development of the people who are showing good potential to be the leaders of the future. We have already identified that every person has the ability to be a leader at some point, but there will be those who are able to demonstrate leadership qualities from an early stage and who should be given every opportunity to develop these.

Every successful organisation will have a programme for the recognition and training of their leaders of the future. They want to select people who have a natural gifting and pour into them all the relevant knowledge and experience of their existing leaders with the intention of equipping them to take the organisation to greater heights than ever before.

(i) Recognising Leadership Traits

It begins with the task of spotting people who are generally younger, fitter, and more energetic, who already exhibit some leadership skills and who have a genuine desire to learn, but care must be exercised at this point so they don't get the impression they are being treated more favourably than others.

It is absolutely clear that some leadership qualities which may be quite evident in some people can be completely absent in others so there is no fixed way of assessing this. The Christian leader needs to be astute in gauging the character as well as the skills of potential leaders before he makes his views known to anyone in order to try to ensure time and energy are not going to be invested inappropriately.

> **It is not necessarily the most gifted people who turn out to be the best leaders, but those who are most willing to learn, grow and be a part of the team.**

Identifying at an early stage those who naturally seem to demonstrate leadership qualities can be a great catalyst for the development of others in the group. It can build a desire for progress, help to lift the morale, and raise the standards of the whole group. When the apostle Paul wrote to the church in Rome he stressed the importance of seeing that, although we are all equal, each person possesses different gifts which need to be recognised and nurtured (Romans 12 v 3 - 5).

(ii) Rehearsing Leadership Talents

Paul goes on to say in Romans 12 v 6 – 9, that once people's gifts have been recognised, we all have a responsibility to create the space for them to exercise their gifts. Making room for people in this way will usually present some serious challenges to the whole group because some positions and responsibilities will need to be adjusted. This is a vital part of encouraging an attitude of maturity in the group and it can help to prevent people becoming too inward looking or losing their focus on the main objectives of the group.

This process is not simply allowing people to do things, but about actually helping people practice their developing gifts and skills and it is an essential role that needs to be exercised by everyone in leadership and practised by everyone in the group. It is one of the patterns we can see that Jesus used when training His disciples and it included several distinct stages, as follows:

> a) watch me do it, b) do it with me, c) do it
> while I watch, d) do it on your own.

This pattern enabled them to witness Jesus doing His work before attempting something similar themselves, and then only under the watchful eye of the Master. It was a pattern for building confidence. Even though their confidence was not to be in their own ability or strength but in the supernatural power of His Holy Spirit, they still needed to learn how to do this without taking any of the glory for themselves – a vital principle in Christian Leadership.

Without opportunities like this to rehearse their gifts in a safe environment it is very difficult for potential leaders to cultivate the right attitude towards their skills. This process allows them to make mistakes and to use these as a means of additional learning before moving on to become the people God can use to develop others.

(iii) Releasing Leadership Transformers

Potential leaders who demonstrate an ability to enable other people to mature and grow need to be released into wider spheres of activity as soon as is practicable. These are the catalysts who can transform whole organisations by working alongside other individuals who want to bring about change. For the Christian leader to release such people too early would be a grave error of judgement, but to hold such people back for too long would be a serious dereliction of duty. However, for a leader to be able to release gifted people in this way it will require him to exercise great courage and have genuine confidence in his own sense of security. Furthermore, it will need to be a principle which is clearly understood and accepted by the whole group.

It should be the very pinnacle of every leader's work – to see the people they have taught, mentored and encouraged begin to step forward in faith and develop their own strategies. The process of 'releasing', actually means having to let people go and watch them start to make their own way while at the same time resisting the temptation to exercise any sort of control over them. Transformers are people who have what it takes to bring Christian Leadership principles to bear in whatever situation they find themselves.

They will possess, and know how to exercise, many of the qualities listed here and will have the character, wisdom and patience to understand that leadership is always a process that begins and ends with people. When people have been brought up on and adopted these principles it is a real honour to see them released into their own avenues of service and it is a massive credit to the leader who has inspired them.

7. Positive & Unwavering Conflict Management

(These Principles of Handling every kind of Distraction and Opposition are taken from the book of Nehemiah in The Bible).

Managing the External Stages of Opposition

(i)	Seriously Disturbing	(Chapter 2 v 10)
(ii)	Mocking and Ridiculing	(Chapter 2 v 19)
(iii)	Anger and Sarcasm	(Chapter 4v 1)
(iv)	Plotting to Take Action	(Chapter 4 v 8)
(v)	Spreading Rumours	(Chapter 4 v 11)
(vi)	Conspiring and Scheming	(Chapter 6 v 2)
(vii)	Lying and Slandering	(Chapter 6 v 6)
(viii)	Buying Support and Manipulating	(Chapter 6 v 13)
(ix)	Intimidating Correspondence	(Chapter 6 v 19)
(x)	Infiltrating the Work	(Chapter 13 v 5)

Handling the Internal Issues of Conflict

(a)	Grievances and Complaints	(Chapter 5 v 1-5)
(b)	Colluding with the Opposition	(Chapter 13 v 7)
(c)	Neglecting Responsibilities	(Chapter 13 v 10)
(d)	Ignoring Spiritual Principles	(Chapter 13 v 17)
(e)	Abandoning Moral Standards	(Chapter 13 v 23)

There are some very important differences between the way External and Internal conflicts should be handled, but the great similarity between them is that there is nearly always a progression in the stages of development amongst people who wish to undermine your project. What starts as something fairly innocent, if not managed appropriately can quickly fester and develop into something extremely serious. We must also realise that, even when issues of conflict are being managed, the perpetrators will rarely be satisfied because their agenda is usually completely different to that of the project. It is the responsibility of the Christian Leader to develop a clear strategy for facing and managing every aspect of conflict as soon as it occurs because any delay in doing this will merely encourage an escalation of the problem.

> *"Conflict is normal ... but it must be understood and managed.*
> *Conflict always produces energy, but this can become the very*
> *resource that can be used for resolving the conflict"*
> (Roxburgh & Romanuk 2020 p134)

In this section we will work through the progression of issues of conflict as they are recorded in the Biblical story of Nehemiah's challenge to rebuild the walls of Jerusalem. Here we can see a classic example of Christian Leadership in action. The background to the story is that the Jews, who had recently returned from exile in Babylon, found the city of Jerusalem had been devastated and the city walls completely broken down. When this was reported to Nehemiah, he immediately began a 4 month period of fasting and prayer before commencing any action. In spite of this, even before he actually arrived at Jerusalem, opposition was already beginning to emerge.

Managing the Stages of External Opposition

(i) Seriously Disturbing (Chapter 2 v 10)

News of the forthcoming arrival of Nehemiah was immediately perceived to be a threat to those who held political office in the region at that time. Even though his intention to rebuild the walls of the city was predominantly practical, they feared that his work would elevate the status of the Jewish people so that the authority of the officials would be brought into question. It was the beginning of their descent into a whole catalogue of negative and destructive responses, although at this point their attitudes had not yet come become public.

It is not uncommon for leaders in all walks of life who are preparing to take up a new challenge to discover that some opposition has started to develop even before they have moved into position. When people are seriously disturbed their murmuring, grumbling and complaining becomes the seedbed from which all kinds of rebellious activities are likely to develop. Christian Leaders need to be aware that there will often be grumblings going on beneath the surface that don't require any attention to be paid to them until such time as they surface. However, spending time with God in prayer is an important way in which God is able to prepare leaders to face these unknowns.

(ii) Mocking and Ridiculing (Chapter 2 v 19)

As soon as the work begins, this is the trigger for the opposition to make themselves known. It will often take the form of mocking and making fun of those who are involved and this can occur for many different reasons such as: from an inaccurate understanding of the project, from a deliberate misinterpretation of the objectives, or for some totally selfish reasons. It will often manifest itself in challenging and sometimes inappropriate questions and accusations which are intended to humiliate the workers and question the validity of the project.

Nehemiah deals with this by choosing neither to be drawn into any discussion nor by responding to their questions or accusations, but instead remaining firmly focused on his rationale for taking on the job. He immediately establishes his allegiance to God and, in doing so he marks out a clear distinction between those who wish to be associated with God's purposes and those who don't.

Christian Leaders should follow this pattern from the outset by avoiding all unnecessary and unhelpful dialogue over possible objections by establishing a clear focus and rationale for their work. Nehemiah refused to take the criticism personally and so was not demoralised in any way by their comments. It actually seemed to confirm that he was doing the right thing and it spurred him on to make certain that his focus was kept in the right place.

(iii) Anger and Sarcasm (Chapter 4 v 1)

At this point, the work was in full swing and progress was becoming obvious, so it seemed to generate an increase in the levels of the reactions coming from the opposition. This often results in the opponents becoming angry and incensed by the work, consequently choosing to make their comments more barbed, critical and personal in front of their own supporters. They love to be seen making their objections publicly and, as it were, parading up and down, playing to the crowd and seeking the approval of the masses.

Nehemiah was not in the least fazed by their posturing or their insults but instead turned immediately to God in prayer. He gave the whole situation to God by asking Him to deal with it so he and his entire workforce could maintain their focus on the work in hand. His example of not being sidetracked by this attack acted as a major motivation for his workers so that they rallied in support behind him. They worked even more enthusiastically and the project moved forward substantially.

Whenever the criticism and verbal attacks increase the Christian leader would do well to increase the fervency and frequency of his prayer times with God rather than attempt to handle these issues himself. This kind of commitment from the leader, and his refusal to be distracted from the work, is likely to consolidate and strengthen the commitment and dedication of the workers which, in turn, can enable the work to gather pace.

(iv) Plotting to Take Action (Chapter 4 v 8)

Seeing the work continue to gather momentum will often increase the frustration levels of the opposition to the point where they decide that some physical action must be taken because their words and verbal assaults are no longer deemed to be having any effect. As their anger continues to rise they begin to plot a confrontation which will stir up additional trouble against the project. This was to be more than just a protest march, they wanted a fight.

This is the stage where people are coming together to pool their resources in order to create a more cohesive attack on the project. Opposition is moving beyond the concept of casually throwing insults, onto a more coordinated attempt at bringing people together for a planned assault. Modern technology makes this process so quick and easy to bring into effect that it can become an almost instant option in many situations.

Nehemiah was not fazed by this development even though he was aware that his workers were tiring in the face of the volume of work that had to be accomplished. He called for a programme of 24 hour prayer and action. Christian leaders must never assume that either one of these will be sufficient on its own because God expects us to be involved in whatever He is doing. Having a prayerful link with God increases the likelihood of making the right choices but there is still a requirement for us to take appropriate action, so the practical involvement of everyone is usually a good move.

(v) Spreading Rumours (Chapter 4 v 11)

The psychological war continued with the opposition beginning to spread false rumours. The specific intention here was to whip up the enthusiasm of the protesters. These rumours and threats were then deliberately leaked to the workers on the project to try to cause panic and undermine their morale. The morale of any group can be a fragile thing which can quickly be disrupted by only one or two people losing focus or getting 'cold feet'. Swift action is therefore required on the part of the leader to prevent morale dropping in this way and to re-invigorate the workers.

Nehemiah immediately posted teams of fully armed warriors at all of the most vulnerable places and built these teams around families so they would fight to the bitter end to defend one another and protect the project. Then he spoke to everyone by reminding them not to be afraid but to put their trust in the supernatural power of Almighty God and to be prepared to fight for their cause.

Because of these threats, Nehemiah decided to change his strategy slightly at this point (v16), by appointing people to specific roles according to their gifting. Some were to act as armed guards so it would enable others to keep their focus on doing the work. In some areas he instructed people to continue working but have their weapons ready at hand in case of a surprise attack, and he instituted an alarm system so that if an attack occurred others would be able to rally to that point immediately. He also showed care and compassion for his workers by providing protection for them night and day so the work would not be hindered.

The Christian Leader needs Godly wisdom to be able to respond whenever there is a crisis by making the right decisions, but this is only likely to happen when he has a strong on-going relationship with The Lord. Making good tactical decisions <u>and</u> inspiring the workers are qualities that come from knowing God's plan and choosing to be at the centre of it. It also involves the ability to demonstrate a caring nature towards those who are committing themselves to work on the project. When these things are put in place it improves the likelihood that the workers will want to return to their tasks and not be put off by external threats.

(vi) Conspiring and Scheming (Chapter 6 v 2)

This stage is a really difficult one to handle and it occurs when the opposition appear to hold out an olive branch by suggesting a meeting on neutral ground to discuss the problem. Nehemiah was not fooled by this approach because he weighed up the character of the opposition by the way they had conducted themselves up to this point and he was able to draw on the supernatural wisdom of God in framing his response.

The opposition knew that if they could remove or incapacitate Nehemiah the whole project would be likely to fail so they made a number of concerted attempts to achieve this (v4). These attempts to get him alone by drawing him away from the work came to nothing because Nehemiah saw through their scheme and refused to comply with their demands. Instead he reminded them of the task to which he was committed and that this was going to remain his priority.

There are likely to be many occasions when the Christian Leader will need to exercise a similar kind of wisdom without showing any animosity whatsoever. It would have been very easy for Nehemiah to want to go on the offensive against his oppressors but he resisted the temptation by maintaining his focus on the work in hand.

(vi) Lying and Slandering (Chapter 6 v 5-7)

Making false accusations and threatening to broadcast these far and wide is yet another devious attempt to get Nehemiah to defend his position by meeting his oppressors in private. It was also their intention to frighten his workers by making them think they were doing something illegal that would have drastic consequences.

They really pulled out all the stops at this point by trying to back their accusations with personal testimony from one of their own number and by deliberately misinterpreting and inventing what the prophets were saying. They were struggling to find others to blame and, knowing Nehemiah's faith, sought also to undermine his trust in the prophets

Nehemiah's reply is brief and to the point (v8) as he dismisses their accusations without further ado but he still refuses to be drawn into any discussion about his motives. He knows that everyone in that area would understand the rationale for this project even if they didn't agree with it. He then turns immediately to prayer and asks God for the strength he needs to complete the work. His prayer is not just for himself but for every person who is involved alongside him in the project.

Every Christian leader is going to experience a variety of attempts to distract him from the work he has taken on and it will require great resolve to avoid being drawn into pursuing all kinds of 'red herrings'. Yet God chooses to use 'red herrings' to test our level of commitment to Him and His purposes. Only when we have the certainty of knowing that we are where God wants us to be and doing what He wants us to be doing can we have the confidence to avoid all such distractions.

(vii) Buying Support and Manipulating (Chapter 6 v 13)

At this point, a seemingly innocent request was received by Nehemiah during one of his pastoral visits to Shemaiah, who was housebound. However, the message through Shemaiah was very similar to the ones he had received before – he suggested a meeting in secret, but this time inside the temple, with the doors closed! The intimation here was that Nehemiah would be afraid to meet openly because Shemaiah was known to be associating with the opposition. He was appealing to Nehemiah's close relationship with God, but it backfired when Nehemiah received a word of knowledge that this man was not sent by God but had been hired by the opposition.

This move by the opposition appears to be giving ground, with a possible desire to compromise by offering to meet on Nehemiah's home territory. They were caught out because of Nehemiah's close walk with God which enabled The Holy Spirit to speak directly into his mind to expose the true motives of Shemaiah. When accurate evidence cannot be found to support the opposition's schemes they can so easily fall into the temptation of trying to buy support. Such manipulation of a person's genuine qualities in order to achieve their own ends is a common failing among people who are opposed to the work of God.

It underlines the absolute necessity for Christian Leaders to develop and maintain a close personal relationship with The Lord at all times and to be filled with The Holy Spirit continuously. It is what enabled Nehemiah to extend the same care and protection to Shemaiah that was being offered to everyone else in the city at that time without any fear for his own safety. It also enabled him to recognise that in spite of Shemaiah being one of many other prophets who were under the influence of the opposition, Nehemiah was still willing to pray for them.

(viii) Intimidating Correspondence (Chapter 6 v 17-19)

It is not unusual to come across situations in life where someone in the opposition is closely related to someone who is working on your project, so when this happens, it should come as no surprise to discover that they want to use this connection to create additional hardship for the leader. In this case, the people who are holding responsible positions and who should know better, are using this tactic to try to undermine the confidence of Nehemiah by sending a stream of letters back and forth even after the project had been completed. Their on-going effort to discredit Nehemiah merely demonstrates their growing fear and lack of allegiance.

The Christian Leader must constantly be alert to the fact that there may well be aspects of intimidation that continue to be carried out under a veneer of respectability. Here Tobiah, who was quite a high ranking official, was consorting with nobles of the tribe of Judah to send letters that praised Tobiah for his good deeds, as a way of trying to intimidate Nehemiah. Nehemiah responded by choosing to completely ignore this approach and simply got on with the tasks of organising what needed to be done next.

(ix) Infiltrating the Work (Chapter 13 v 5)

When all else fails, the opposition may try to infiltrate the work in an attempt to undermine the project from the inside. In this instance they chose the wrong man – Tobiah – because he was well known to Nehemiah and therefore easily identifiable. What is most worrying about this incident is the fact that this had been made possible by the man, Eliashib, who had been entrusted by Nehemiah with the task of managing the store rooms. Eliashib had been manipulated by Tobiah into letting him have the use of some of the rooms that were originally set aside for the storage of provisions for those who served in the temple.

Apart from the fact God had previously made public that anyone who was an Ammonite was specifically banned from having access to the temple (13 v 1), Eliashib would have known that Tobiah was an arch-enemy of the work Nehemiah was doing and this, therefore, made this a failure of the highest order. As soon as it was discovered, Nehemiah took immediate action: he threw out all of Tobiah's possessions, he ordered the rooms to be sanitised, he sacked Eliashib, he ordered all the equipment and provisions for the temple to be put back into the rooms where it belonged and he appointed a team of three people to manage the job from this point on.

When serious breaches of trust are discovered the Christian Leader must be able to take immediate action to rectify the situation because blatant rebellion of this nature should never be tolerated. This conveys a vital message to everyone involved in the work of the project that when any opposition to agreed standards is carried out publicly, the retribution will also be handled publicly.

In all of the preceding stages of opposition Nehemiah hardly bothers to respond to his assailants, choosing instead to pour out his heart to God in prayer each time. But when a flagrant disregard for principles becomes evident, which could put the whole project in jeopardy, he must be expected to restore those principles immediately. The greatest challenge for the Christian Leader is to be able to do this with poise and grace, without displaying any anger or vindictiveness. Nehemiah gives us a wonderful example of how this can be achieved.

<u>Handling the Issues of Internal Conflict</u>

(a) Grievances and Complaints (Chapter 5 v 1-5)

From time to time every leader is likely to come across issues of genuine grievance which will require his attention. These will usually be issues that can have a negative effect on the performance of his followers and so he will need to find the time to address these as soon as possible in order to prevent them destroying the morale of the group and becoming a distraction from the work.

Nehemiah was made aware of a number of issues where some of his followers were taking advantage of others who were less well off and were treating them unfairly. He was immediately able to relate to the problem and quickly called everyone together to deal with the difficulties. He spoke frankly and openly to everyone by pointing out exactly where their standards had slipped and setting out what needed to be done to correct these. Furthermore, he explained that there would be serious repercussions for anyone who failed in this.

Once the people had agreed to his directions Nehemiah called together the people who had the job of overseeing the work and commissioned them to ensure that what everyone had agreed to would be carried out. Then he continued to demonstrate his own attitude of generosity towards others by inviting people to dine with him every day at his own expense.

Every Christian Leader must be aware that the way in which he models the standards and principles he speaks about will convey a very powerful message to his followers. Someone once said:

"What you are speaks so loudly that people don't hear what you say"

The level of generosity and care that the Christian Leader is willing to express towards others around him, without losing focus on the work being done, will create a lasting impression upon everyone and become a strong motivation for the whole group going forward.

(b) Colluding with the opposition (Chapter 13 v 7)

On one occasion, after Nehemiah had been away for a while, he discovered one of the leaders that he had appointed was involved in colluding with the opposition. Eliashib had been persuaded to invite someone who was strongly opposed to their work to take up residence in one of the rooms that were specifically allocated for the storage of important items relating to the project. It is impossible to imagine why he thought this would be a good idea so it can only be assumed that either he had completely lost his vision for the project or he was being bribed.

It is not unusual, whenever the leader stops proclaiming, teaching and modelling the vision, for people to begin to drift in their understanding and application of its principles. This is what will allow access to the enemy and which will begin to undermine and destroy the work (compare 1 Corinthians 5 v 6 – 8). The seriousness of such behaviour must never be underestimated and so immediate and decisive action is required to counter such an event. Nehemiah removed Eliashib from office, restored the rooms to their original purpose, and introduced a different system to try to prevent such an event from happening again.

When people in positions of responsibility (leaders) show they are not in tune with the overall vision of the project, it is essential that they are removed from office as quickly as possible. Of course, it is vital that the Christian Leader doesn't jump to conclusions without knowing the facts, or act inappropriately, but failing to act would amount to a serious dereliction of duty.

(c) Neglecting Responsibilities (Chapter 13 v 10)

Every person in any position of leadership has an on-going need for support and encouragement. When this is not forthcoming even the strongest and most dedicated leaders can lose their focus and fail to maintain their role effectively. In this passage the work of the temple was being neglected because the officials (leaders) were neglecting their responsibilities by not rewarding people as they should have been.

In situations like this the morale of the whole group can begin to drop quickly because it looks as though the leaders really don't care anymore. They become too occupied with other issues and start to neglect the main role that was entrusted to them so that the whole project begins to suffer. For this reason it is always best to appoint leaders to be part of a team and not to be isolated or on their own. This will give them the very best chance of developing their skill and maturity by remaining efficient and conscientious at all times.

As soon as Nehemiah learned the extent of the problem he rebuked those who had let him down, he got them to return to their posts and then he appointed a new team over them. Christian Leadership always involves bringing on and developing the leaders of the future but we must recognise that we still have a responsibility to teach and encourage those who have failed.

(d) Ignoring Spiritual Principles (Chapter 13 v 17)

The Christian Leader must always be aware of the dangers of allowing the standards of the world to creep into his work instead of continuing to operate by the standards of The Bible. In Nehemiah's day God had given specific instructions in the Law of Moses that the Sabbath was to be protected as a day set apart for worship, so work of any sort was strictly prohibited on this day. Consequently when Nehemiah saw that people had begun working, trading and dealing on the Sabbath day he immediately put a stop to it and even banned from entering the city those who were not bound by the Sabbath regulations.

Whenever standards start to slip it is the leader's responsibility to take swift action to rectify the slide. It is quite easy to get so caught up in the development or expansion of the work that people begin to overlook the maintenance of important standards. It must be recognised that standards and practices which may be widely acceptable to the world in general may not be acceptable if Biblical principles are to be maintained. There is a fine line between the two and the Christian Leader must be constantly alert to any attempts to compromise here.

In the language of today this might require the Christian Leader to introduce a clear statement of faith, to develop specific aims and objectives for the projects on which he is working, and to set out specifically anything that would not be acceptable to the standards expected within the project. However enthusiastic the followers may be they cannot be expected to maintain standards of which they are unaware or which have not been comprehensively communicated.

(e) Abandoning Moral Standards (Chapter 13 v 23-28)

In order to protect the heritage of the Children of Israel, God had laid down specific instructions about the nations with whom they were not allowed to inter-marry and that any who chose to step outside this ruling needed to be expelled and treated as outcasts. Nehemiah took swift and strong action against those who had offended in this way and made them promise publicly that they would not allow similar errors of judgement to be made in the future.

Although this sounds excessively harsh in today's parlance, we must understand that many of the promises God made to them were conditional upon their willingness to be obedient. Every leader should take great care to research and understand what standards may be a requirement of his organisation and what his own position is in regard to maintaining these.

The Christian Leader must be absolutely crystal clear, with every person before they get involved in any aspect of his project, about any standards of moral behaviour that will be required of them, what the reasons are for this, and what consequences may ensue if they choose to transgress. Followers and participants must be in no doubt about these requirements and must make it clear that they have understood and agree to abide by these standards before beginning any work for the project. This, effectively forms a contract without which, it will be extremely difficult, even impossible, for the leader to exercise any authority in this regard.

The benefit of this is that once appropriate standards are in place and have been accepted (where appropriate, contracts have been signed), any person who then chooses to ignore these will be making their own decision that they no longer wish to be involved in the work of the project.

8. Determined & Diligent Personal Sacrificing

(i)   Suppressing the Ego – Honest in Self Deprecation
(ii) Submitting to Others – Wholesome in Self Denial
(iii) Surrendering to God – Humble in Self Discipline

The whole issue of self-sacrifice, although it is an essential quality for the Christian Leader, must be kept in a right balance. Where this is not done it is likely to result in a growing sense of pride and arrogance, and where it is overemphasised it can produce workaholics who allow the erosion of standards, justify the neglecting of responsibilities, and easily lose sight of the main objectives.

Christians are often worse than other people in this respect because they can feel that it is their duty to sacrifice themselves in the service of The Lord. Many feel there is something almost 'super-spiritual' about this kind of self suppression and they can consequently get easily caught up in a spiral of over-commitment.

However good a quality may be, if it is carried to an extreme, it will become a negative and destructive quality.

(i) Suppressing the Ego – Honest in Self Deprecation

The Bible makes it clear that in order to live the Christian life effectively we are required, by The Holy Spirit, to bring our old nature under control so that it can no longer dictate our thoughts and behaviours (Romans 8 v 1-13). For every person this will need a willingness to be blatantly honest with themselves if any progress is to be made in this respect. Old habits die hard, and it is no easy task to keep our old nature out of the limelight so we can remain sensitive to the more subtle promptings and guidance of The Holy Spirit (John 3 v 30).

Every Christian Leader needs to develop ways of regularly keeping a check on the status of their own ego, especially in regard to their role of leadership. This will help prevent any confusion between their ability to make good decisions and their inherent desire to promote themselves. Keeping the ego in check is not about comparing ourselves with others, but it is about a reality check over whose best interests are being served by the choices, decisions and actions we are making. To do this effectively we must scrutinise every detail of our behaviour before God and to ensure that we don't cut any corners, this is best done along with a personal friend or mentor who will be totally honest with us.

The biggest difficulty with believing that we can do this without the help of anyone else is that we can easily convince ourselves that every single action we take is being done purely for the benefit of others. ("The human heart is deceitful above all things" - Jeremiah17 v 9). There is a very fine line between taking pride in what we are doing, and being proud. Few leaders have really learned the art of being blatantly honest with themselves and therefore, not only will they struggle with this concept but, unless it is tackled with complete honesty, they will discover their followers beginning to adopt similar tendencies.

The degree to which leaders are effective with this exercise will frequently determine the success of their whole leadership role. Many leaders, including Christians, have fallen from high positions because they were unable or unwilling to subject themselves to this kind of scrutiny. Many leadership tragedies, and damage to a great many followers, could have been avoided if a process like this had been consistently applied to their work. The suppressing of the ego is massively significant for every Christian Leader and will continue to be significant in keeping each of the other aspects of personal sacrifice in perspective.

(ii) Submitting to Others – Wholesome in Self Denial

This is another element that many leaders find extremely difficult to put into practice. It is a common mistake, even for Christian Leaders, to believe they are above the need to submit to others, yet The Bible states clearly that we are all required to submit to one another (Ephesians 5 v 21), and it seems to me there can be no exceptions to that.

Submission is always a personal choice and is therefore an act of self denial. I may choose to submit to a person to allow them to speak into my life or to give them authority over me for a particular reason or during a particular activity. That is never intended to lock me into a life-long commitment of submission, but is meant for that time, season, or situation. Within the Christian church we are all required to submit to one another at different times and for different reasons according to the gifts and responsibilities people are exercising at that time. This is what makes 'the body' effective.

Some Christian Leaders however, have been known to quote Hebrews 13 v 17 to their flock, (which says "Obey your leaders and submit to their authority...") in order to justify the need for everyone to continually submit to them. Unfortunately they miss the important principle here of submitting to those who are leading us, or guiding us, at that point and this relates to the principle that we all have something to learn from one another. For any leader to be able to do this deliberately and with good grace is a mark of high quality.

Any leader who is unable or unwilling to choose to submit to the authority of other people at certain times and for specific reasons, is simply indicating their lack of suitability to be a leader.

(iii) Surrendering to God – Humble in Self Discipline

It is quite likely that any leader who is not able to suppress their own ego and submit to other people is going to find it incredibly difficult to surrender to God, yet this is the challenge for every Christian whether or not they are involved in any aspect of leadership (Hebrews 12 v 9). It becomes especially important for the Christian Leader because without this he will inevitably be operating primarily in his own strength.

Surrendering to God does not mean abandoning the ability to think and reason, nor is it about blindly following Biblical principles. It must be a conscious choice which is made willingly and from a genuine desire to be obedient to the teachings of The Bible. However, personal surrender does involve allowing God to dictate the decisions we make about every aspect of our life, and this amounts to three elements:- a) Everything I am, b) Everything I have, and c) Everything I desire.

a)   Everything I am. This includes everything about me – my health, my talents, my skills, my abilities and inabilities, my moods, my positive and my negative qualities, the roles and responsibilities I have such as father, husband, brother, child, and so on, all the positions I hold, my attitudes and prejudices, my successes and failures, my fears and phobias, my likes and dislikes, my strengths and weaknesses.

b)   Everything I have. This includes all my possessions such as; house, car, boat, business, clothes, valuables, jewellery, equipment, property, heirlooms, all money, bank accounts, investments, all stocks and shares, anything held in trust, as well as all debts.

c)   Everything I desire. This is whatever I wish to see in the future, including; my dreams, my plans, my wishes, the things I hope for or long for or have worked for, whether for myself, for those whom I love, for those with whom I work, or for other people.

In order for me to be serious about my need to surrender, I must be willing to take my hands off all these things and lay them at the feet of God by inviting Him to give me His guidance and direction as to how I should handle these from now on. Surrender involves acknowledging the absolute sovereignty of God in every circumstance whether good, bad, or indifferent and accepting that He has a plan to bring about His purposes through every situation.

There is a progression here which involves all of these elements in order to understand the true meaning of self sacrifice. Every one of these elements has a bearing on each of the others but it is only when they are all in place that the Christian Leader will be able to appreciate the importance of self sacrifice.

9. Dependable and Inspirational Supporting

(i)   Honour in Serving Individuals
(ii)   Hope in Strengthening Individuals
(iii)   Happiness in Supervising Individuals

The on-going support and encouragement of the people who have been fellow workers and followers is another mark of a good leader. Without this it would be easy for people to believe they have been used by their leader merely to achieve his own purposes. In the Bible, the apostle Paul frequently shows concern for the people who have worked alongside him, for example in; 2 Timothy 4 v 19-21, in Titus 2 v 12-13, and in the whole of Romans chapter 16. This quality makes a leader stand out as someone who is genuine in his concern for people.

(i) Honour in Serving Individuals

The Christian Leader will be someone who counts it as a real honour to have the privilege of serving others (Matthew 20 v 26-28). The greatest challenges with these are; a) the need to achieve the overall purpose for the leader's calling whilst, b) at the same time helping his followers achieve their own objectives and then c) continuing to support and encourage them as they go beyond the vision of the leader.

Serving, is meeting other people's needs and it requires a high level of humility if it is to be carried out effectively. This appears to cut right across the role of leadership yet Jesus made it abundantly clear that there is no conflict here. You simply cannot call yourself a Christian Leader if you are unwilling to see your service of other people as a necessary part of your role.

We must also understand here that serving individuals is completely different to serving an organisation. There may be a certain amount of honour and acclaim attached to serving an organisation and, they may wish to publicise and draw attention to this, but the honour that comes from serving individuals will be very different. It will result in a deep inner sense of satisfaction that will far surpass any form of public recognition.

(ii) Hope in Strengthening Individuals

It is essential for the Christian Leader to be able to look beyond what their followers may be able to achieve in the present and to help them grasp a greater vision for their potential in the future. This is real leadership and, although it may involve some aspect of specific training and development, it will always include the need for the leader to pour into his followers generous amounts of unconditional positive regard.

The Christian Leader must be able to balance this kind of time consuming work carefully so as neither to show any favouritism, nor to neglect the wider concerns of the project. Great leaders are those who build up and empower their followers to achieve greater things in the future than they ever thought possible. Hope, in the Biblical sense, is holding onto the certainty of what people are capable of achieving through the strength God provides.

It will often involve an amount of gentle pushing and persuasion but this must be handled sensitively and not overdone or it will backfire by generating more problems for the individuals within the group. This could be cited by the leader as a reason for not doing this in the first place, but that is just an excuse and should not be entertained by the Christian

Leader. Jesus often prompted His disciples to step out in faith whilst He was still available to support them (Matthew 14 v 16).

(iii) Happiness in Supervising Individuals

There is real joy attached to seeing people grow and move on in their gifts and abilities and this can continue when there is an opportunity for the leader to offer on-going supervision to people. When they move outside the responsibility of the leader, some may wish to retain their connection by asking to be supervised, or mentored, or coached in order to continue their development.

In the days when I was playing table-tennis, I found one thing to be so much more satisfying than winning my own matches, and it was watching the young people I had trained go on to reach greater heights than me. It is difficult to explain, but the satisfaction for the Christian Leader in continuing to supervise the people he helped initially, and see them take great strides forward, will far surpass any satisfaction he gained from his own achievements.

Supervision, in this context, will frequently be a kind of coaching role in which the leader is continuing to urge people to break new ground, to pioneer new developments and techniques, or simply to grow in their own application of the principles they have already learned. It is like helping people onto another level, to develop, mature, and fly! When Jesus saw the sense of excitement and fulfilment that was expressed by His disciples when they returned from a mission, Luke described His response as experiencing "wild ecstatic joy through The Holy Spirit" (Luke 10 v 21).

10. Continuous & Strategic Progressing

(i)   Constructing a Team
(ii)   Creating a Template
(iii) Cultivating an Trajectory

The final essential quality we will consider here is all to do with what legacy the Christian Leader will leave behind. What are the lasting impressions that have been made on the people, and what is the evidence that Christian Leadership has been effective? Ultimately we will not be judged on the success of the project(s) we have undertaken, but on the quality of the lives that have been changed under our influence, and on the strategies we have introduced that will enable people to continue to grow towards maturity in the future.

The success of Jesus' ministry was not to do with how many people He healed, the number of places where he preached, how long He held His office, how many people He delivered from evil spirits, or even how many people followed Him throughout His time on earth. It was all to do with what He left behind when He departed this life. It was all to do with the strategies He put in place to encourage people to grow into spiritual maturity in the future. That was, and still is, His legacy of continuous and strategic progression.

(i) Constructing a Team.

The Christian Leader should have a clear intention, right from the outset, of building a team to undertake whatever work he is called to do. The Biblical concept of team is established right from the beginning of The Bible (Genesis 1 v 1-3), where we see Father, Son and Holy Spirit working together in total harmony. This was further emphasised when God created mankind as body, soul and spirit (Genesis 1 v 26, and 1 Thessalonians 5 v 23).

All the way through The Bible we can see the importance God places on building team. Whenever He appoints a leader, He expects him to quickly build a team around him (Exodus 18 v 25) who he will train to be the future leaders. This is perfectly demonstrated in the life of Jesus who, right at the start of His ministry, pulled together a group of disciples and then began building them into a team. After this, throughout the New Testament, whenever a church was started it was established by a team of people.

Teams are God's methods of building. We can see this emphasised through the book of Ephesians where the apostle Paul speaks about the church as a body (or team), each part with different roles and responsibilities yet working together in perfect harmony. This should be the pattern for every group or organisation under Christian Leadership.

There will be some cases where leaders may not get to choose their own team, particularly in the first instance. For example in the government the Prime Minister cannot always choose who will be available to him, but he still has the responsibility to train and mould his people into a working team. Every Christian Leader, in whatever situation they find themselves, should be committed to constructing a team of people around him and then working to mould them together as a unit. This will convey a vital message that, although the work may be important, it is the people who are the most important part of the work

(ii) Creating a Template

This aspect of Christian Leadership goes beyond simply constructing a team, to developing a pattern that can be reproduced throughout the whole organisation. The objective here is to demonstrate such strong principles within the team that they will automatically begin to be copied throughout the whole organisation and the way it operates. The intention is that every person would see the benefits of this style of working and want to adopt similar ways of doing things. When each section or department in the organisation begins to take on similar patterns of operating, it is possible to see a culture beginning to emerge.

It is not so much the responsibility of the individual group leader to achieve this, nor should it be the specific intention of his team, but when people in the wider organisation witness the effectiveness of this style of operating it is likely they will want to utilise a similar pattern. When the leaders of other sections or departments can see the potential to improve their ways of working, and the effect this can have on their own team members, the principles can catch on really quickly.

It usually takes a long while to get to the stage where everyone in an organisation understands and accepts a certain approach to working and where people share the same standards and values, but when this happens it produces a sense of harmony and unity which can lift the whole atmosphere so that people become more dedicated and conscientious, the quality of the work improves and things get done more efficiently.

When leaders throughout the organisation begin to adapt and modify these processes whilst continuing to work to similar standards, this becomes the accepted and normal way of doing things. It will then tend to reduce areas of conflict or disagreement and enable differences of opinion to be resolved more easily. Communication improves, there is a better flow of information in all directions and people are proud to be associated with the work.

(iii) Cultivating a Trajectory

This is where the reputation of these ways of working gathers momentum beyond the organisation itself into the wider community. People in other organisations and areas of work begin to notice the methods and standards which are being applied and want to emulate them. They become aware of the way in which the workers or followers are being treated and they can see the obvious benefits attached to this so that Christian standards of leadership are seen as the way to move forward.

This will inevitably begin to challenge and change the widely accepted worldly ways of doing things such as:-

- grabbing as much responsibility as you can to show how important you are instead of consistently giving it away,
- putting other people down in order to gain status instead of promoting the skills and abilities of others,
- bragging about self accomplishments as a way of gaining recognition instead of giving the credit to the team,
- keeping a position as sole leader in order to maintain control instead of nurturing and training a whole brood of exciting new leaders.
- maintaining focus on a personal vision that demonstrates personal ambition instead of expanding the vision of the organisation.

When teams are moulded together according to Christian Leadership principles and these principles become widely adopted and applied within the organisation it will almost certainly get noticed by other leaders and organisations who will then be motivated to want to apply similar principles for themselves. Christian Leadership principles are intended for the growth and development of individuals as well as groups and organisations. They encourage a constant upward trend of advancement and progression which aims to meet the needs of everyone involved. Therefore good, positive, and successful standards of operation will always generate interest from other leaders and groups because these are the marks of a good Christian Leader.

PART 5

CONCLUSIONS

Conclusions

Although the majority of this book has been written from a male perspective, I wish to make it absolutely clear that people should be appointed to leadership roles because of their character and gifting and not because of their gender. There are many situations in every facet of life where people have been inappropriately appointed to positions of leadership simply because they are male and I believe such decisions in any organisation are inexcusable.

Unfortunately, the Peter Principle is still alive and active in many organisations today. This was outlined in the book by Dr Lawrence J Peter in 1969 where he explained that people are frequently appointed to the level of their incompetence. This happens when people, who may have been very successful in one particular role, are assumed to be able to operate at a higher level and are consequently appointed without any further assessment or training. Although this doesn't always happen, a situation can often occur where leaders and authority figures are appointed by a vote of the members which often makes this nothing more than a popularity contest.

There are plenty of other situations where people have muscled themselves into positions of leadership, often because of their own cravings for power or authority, perhaps by exercising the 'gift of the gab' to convince others of their suitability for the job, and/or as a result of demonstrating their ability to be ruthless by treading on as many other people as possible on their journey. Even people who may have been highly successful at something can often convince others (and themselves) that they automatically have what it takes to move into a more responsible position.

The above examples are anathema to true Christian Leadership

Let me remind you that Christian Leadership principles can work for every leader with every people-group in every sphere of life regardless of their faith. You don't have to be a Christian to apply many of the principles of Christian Leadership, but it will make a massive difference if you are.

Until your human spirit is regenerated by God's Holy Spirit you won't be able to discern His voice or know His guidance, you won't be able to draw upon His resources or experience His empowering, and you won't be able to receive His protection from the forces of evil that seek to attack and undermine you every day. So deciding to live the Christian life is really the very first vital step in preparing to be a Christian Leader.

In addition to this, you must not overlook the fact that once you decide to stand and to operate as a Christian Leader you will become a target in ways that never happened to you prior to this. There will be a great many more people who will want to shoot you down in flames, partly because they will be afraid of being challenged by the principles you stand for and partly because they will hate what you believe. With this in mind, let me encourage you, if you haven't already done so, to make a personal confession of faith that will launch you forward on the pathway towards true Christian Leadership (see Appendix A).

For those who may like a more comprehensive outline of the rationale for embarking upon the Christian life, let me suggest that you work your way along 'The Roman Road' (see Appendix B). However, I must emphasise that these are both ways of beginning the journey, the real work of living the Christian life, like that of being a Christian Leader, is something that must continue to be paramount for every minute of every day. Even then, to survive and prosper as a Christian, leaders need to be filled with The Holy Spirit. J. Oswald Saunders, in his book 'Spiritual Leadership' referred to this as "The Indispensible Requirement".

For many people that may sound like a terrible pressure and something to which they are unwilling to commit. The truth is, if you want to be a successful Christian Leader you cannot compromise on the spiritual requirements. In reality, this is no more arduous a requirement than the effort you might put in to maintaining your physical well-being, such as good eating, sleeping, exercising and resting. Without any one of these you would quickly become unable to function, so the Christian Leader must decide to make these spiritual qualities an equally important part of his daily routine.

It makes sense, therefore, for any group, organisation or business, when considering the appointment of anyone to a position of leadership, to first of all review their spiritual credentials. It is what is referred to in

"The Missional Leader" as 'Leadership Readiness Factors' (Roxburgh & Romanuk 2020), and includes testing people's Character, Capacity, Calling and Competency before they are appointed rather than just assuming they are ready. Many catastrophies of leadership would be avoided if candidates were assessed more thoroughly prior to taking up their role, and if clearer boundaries, guidelines and review processes were put in place to help them maintain their well-being once they have started.

Too many interviews for important leadership positions tend to focus on the skills and experience that may be required for the work that needs to be done rather than on the person's ability to develop a sustainable personal and corporate strategy. To focus on either one of these without the other is likely to end in disappointment, so clearly a more balanced emphasis here would be most beneficial for all parties concerned. What also should never be overlooked as a leadership necessity is the strength and depth of the person's personal support network along with their overall personal aims and objectives.

For the Christian Leader there is no substitute for having an uncompromising faith in the supernatural qualities of Almighty God. The assurance this brings, especially in times of crisis, is immeasurable and, the one thing of which you can be absolutely certain is that there will be times of crisis. Leadership is a delicate balancing act, like walking a tightrope, with huge potential pitfalls on either side and, as with every kind of balancing act, it depends on two major components; maintaining concentration on specific areas of focus that will move you forward, whilst at the same time maintaining a wide peripheral awareness. Distractions of all sorts will come flying at you from all directions so slips, trips and falls will be an inevitable part of the learning process. When these happen, survival will depend upon a determination to get up and carry on without being sidetracked from your original mission.

The delicate balancing act of Christian Leadership can also be likened to learning the skill of Windsurfing. This involves a continuous sensitivity to the subtle changes in the direction and force of both the wind and the waves and a realisation that whatever you encountered yesterday is likely to be totally different for today. For someone who is a snow-skier, the ability to remain in balance while everything around you is constantly changing, is referred to as 'Dynamic Balance' and this is a good analogy for the Christian Leader. In all these examples, even the slightest lack of concentration can result in disastrous consequences.

Dr Stephen Olford was the founder of The Institute for Christian Leadership and The Institute for Biblical Preaching in Memphis, USA in 1988. He maintained that no Christian Leader is going to stay upright for very long without a daily personal relationship with The Lord Jesus Christ and whatever he may achieve is only likely to have any lasting effect if it is done in and through the strength of Christ. His life-long slogan was;

**"Only one life, 'twill soon be past, only
what's done for Christ will last"**

His message is summed up in the words of a hymn he wrote which was sung at many of his conventions and conferences.

LORD MEET MY NEED

Lord search my life in every part, reveal the sins that make me fail,
'Til with a broken, contrite heart, I kneel before You to prevail.

Lord cleanse my life from every stain, as I confess my sins to You,
Let no unholy thought remain, 'til I am free, Your work to do.

Lord take my life what e're the price, my self, my gifts my body too,
And through this 'living sacrifice', empower my life, Your will to do.

Lord fill my life with heavenly grace, that I may demonstrate Your love,
'Til I see in every heart and face, Your joy reflected from above.

Lord use my life to reach the lost, on friendly ground or hostile soil,
But never let me count the cost, to live for You in faithful toil.

Lord hear my prayer I humbly plead,
And in Your mercy meet my need.

Adapted from S. F. Olford and P. F. Liljestrand(1970).
Cited in Phillips J (1995)

The ability to stay focused on the tasks ahead, in spite of being attacked from all sides, is a difficult lesson for any leader to learn but one that is essential for their survival. John Casson, in his article in Stress News (2008), called it 'Building Leadership Resilience'. He identified a wide range of qualities which would pre-dispose any leader to be better equipped to stand against the onslaught of opposition which has so frequently destroyed good leaders in the past. Some might describe this as developing a thick skin, but it is so much more than this because leaders who become outwardly hardened can easily lose all their inner sensitivity. Alternatively, if Christian Leaders merely become ultra-sensitive they run the risk of losing their respect and their ability to make tough decisions and to weather tough storms.

> **The Christian Leader really needs to have the hide of a rhinoceros and the heart of a dove. This is what we might refer to as 'spiritual maturity'**

Christian Leaders need to be bold and strong without sacrificing their ability to remain aware of the subtle changes and needs of the people around them. Jesus, who was strong and decisive enough to throw everyone out of temple (John 2 v 13-16), was the same man who shed tears at the tomb of Lazarus (John 11 v 33-35); the man who stood firm against the criticism of the Pharisees (Matthew 23 v 13), was the same man who showed compassion and gentleness towards two men who were blind (Matthew 20 v 34).

Of course, we recognise that He was the Son of God, but He was also completely human and His spiritual maturity started to show when He was only 12 years old while sitting with the teachers in the temple, listening and asking them questions (Luke 2 v 46-47). No wonder they were amazed at the levels of His understanding, yet this was just a beginning because we are told that He continued to grow in wisdom and stature and in favour with God and men (Luke 2 v 52). Here is a perfect example of what we should look for in all potential Christian Leaders.

When Peter was first called as a disciple of Jesus he was a hardened outdoor labourer who was afraid of nothing, but before he could become a leader of the New Testament church he needed to receive the gentleness that comes from The Holy Spirit. It is the combination of these two qualities, and their appropriate application, which mark out Christian Leadership as being different from all other approaches. The real difference in these examples is made possible only by the wisdom and anointing that comes from The Holy Spirit and from being in close constant union with The Heavenly Father.

When there was a problem with the fair distribution of food amongst the body of believers in the early church, the apostles gave specific instructions about the appointment of a team of people to do the job (Acts 6 v 1-3). But it is interesting that the people they were told to look for were neither those who had knowledge of the food industry nor those who had experience in the distribution industry, but those who "are known to be full of The Spirit and wisdom" (v3). Here is a clear directive about the criteria that should be used when considering the appointment of anyone as a Christian Leader.

The Bible reminds us that there are only two kinds of wisdom; that which is spiritual and comes directly from God, and that which is earthly, unspiritual and comes from the devil (James 3 v 15-17). In other words, the wisdom we use will either draw us closer to God or take us further away from Him. It would appear that, as human beings, we are inherently foolish and don't really possess any wisdom of our own. We must be careful, therefore, not to be confused by the world's understanding of wisdom which could be summed up as 'having learned a lot of things', because regardless of how much we have learned from experience we cannot, of ourselves, break out of our human limitations.

The book of Proverbs regularly urges us to seek after and pursue wisdom, and God, in His generosity offers us wisdom as a free gift through His Holy Spirit. His purpose is that we might no longer see things only from a horizontal perspective but that we might see everything from a different perspective, a vertical perspective, a spiritual perspective – His perspective. The apostle Paul confirms this when he writes "And God raised us up with Christ and seated us with Him in the heavenly realms" (Ephesians 2 v 6).

The Christian Leader should be someone who strives to be a person of high integrity at all times. In this regard, one aspect which is fraught with danger, and about which we must most careful, is ensuring we do not use the resources of the organisation for our own purposes without specific approval being received. It is so easy to cross the line in this respect, but when we do, it is likely to produce drastic consequences – see Isaiah 22 v 14-19. Another important part of demonstrating integrity is teaching and explaining to people what Christian Leadership is and why it is different from secular approaches. Unless we do this consistently, people will weigh us against the standards of the world because they have been surrounded by these all their lives.

The Christian Leader must know how to win the loyalty of others and must know how to delegate and be a team player (Verwer 2019). Christian Leadership is always a team activity and should never be dependent upon the initiatives and resources of only one person. However, it is clearly the responsibility of the Christian Leader to introduce such a system then continue to work to ensure that it is maintained. Team systems frequently fail because of the impatience of the leader. It is much quicker and easier for them to make the decisions themselves rather than having to consult others in the team about every little thing. Such an attitude will always lead to a more dictatorial style and will demonstrate that they haven't been willing to put in sufficient time to create a team structure in which the processes of decision making have been discussed, agreed and shared with everyone in advance.

As I write this, we are in the throes of mourning the death of Queen Elizabeth the second of Great Britain – Elizabeth the Great. It is being suggested that she was one of the greatest leaders of our time, yet many people are questioning what exactly she did throughout her life and why we even need a monarchy. It is only since her death that we are beginning to discover the myriads of ways in which she cared both for people, regardless of their background, nationality, or status, for her environment, wherever she set foot, and to recognise that she was one of the finest examples of true Christian Leadership.

We are only just beginning to understand something of the influence she had on politicians, lawmakers, and people in authority, not just in this country but in every nation of the world, and some of the steps she took to inspire cleaner, more efficient ways of living for everyone. We are only just beginning to hear about the gracious advice and support she gave to everyone in her employ and the guidance and wisdom she exercised in her negotiations and discussions at both national and international level. We are only just beginning to know about the ways she was able to bring people together from very different opinions and cultures and how she was able to treat everyone she met with dignity and respect regardless of their background. We are only just beginning to be aware of how she went out of her way to develop and improve aspects of farming, land management and wildlife preservation, and how she pioneered many energy saving principles.

In spite of her tireless commitment to serve others, it didn't protect her from times of great trauma, disappointment and heartache, nor from periods when her family chose to ignore her standards and go their own way. Yet she always managed to reach out to people who were suffering and in distress and demonstrated an empathic connection with those who were experiencing hard times and she never complained or bemoaned her lot and she never criticised or blamed anyone. Whilst she never made any secret of her troubles, she never highlighted these or drew unnecessary attention to them.

So much of her work was done behind the scenes and out of sight yet, as far as I am concerned, these are the very qualities that mark her out to be one of the greatest leaders of all time. I also believe it is no coincidence at all that she did not refrain from telling the world that her life of true service was modelled and sustained by her faith in the person of Jesus Christ. That, my friends, is true Christian Leadership.

**"People of loving service are rare in any walk of life.
Leaders of loving service are rarer, but in all cases those
who serve will be loved and remembered when those who
cling to power and privileges are long forgotten"**
(The Most Revd Justin Wellby, Archbishop of Canterbury, at
the funeral of Queen Elizabeth II. 19th September 2022).

Finally, here is a personal pledge which could be used as a guide for anyone who is involved in any aspect of Christian Leadership to challenge themselves and evaluate how they have been doing over the past few weeks or months. I would encourage everyone, even those who may aspire to be

Christian Leaders, to read, ponder and commit to something like this on a regular basis:

1. I will learn to discern God's plan in everything and not simply react to people, circumstances or situations.
2. I will demonstrate that I have time to think and to listen both to God and to others and respond with an appropriate level of confidentiality.
3. I will play down my detailed specialist function and learn to concentrate on managing the interface between my function and those of others.
4. I will learn to take an integrated overview of the performance of each individual, of my organisation as a whole, and of my role within it.
5. I will improve my ability to delegate to, and to coach, others so they can develop and use their gifts more effectively for the common good.
6. I will regularly give individuals support and encouragement and will seek to do this whenever and wherever opportunities arise.
7. I will constantly seek to broaden my horizons and roles so that I become more compassionate, caring, and empathic towards others.
8. I will learn to become more competent at maintaining a balance between exercising my gifts and fulfilling my responsibilities in leadership.
9. I will work towards reaching an appropriate balance between achieving and nurturing, and will constantly seek to model this to others.
10. I will make decisions in an open and honest manner whilst recognising my responsibility to build and develop relationships with each individual, with my organisation, and with the wider community.

Adapted from *"The Learning Organisation"* by Bob Garratt (2000)

References and Bibliography

Adair J. (1987)	*Effective Teambuilding*	Pan Books. London
Adair J. (1988)	*Effective Leadership*	Pan Books. London
Adair J. (1997)	*Effective Leadership Masterclass*	Pan Books. London
Adair J. (1998)	*Handbook of Management and Leadership*	Thorogood. London
Adair J. (2001)	*The Leadership of Jesus – its Legacy for Today*	Canterbury Press. Norwich
Adair J. (2002)	*Inspiring Leadership – Learning from Great Leaders*	Thorogood. London
Adair J. (2003) 3rd Edition	*Not Bosses, but Leaders – the Way to Success*	Thorogood. London
Adair J. (2003)	*Time management and Personal Development*	Thorogood. London
Adair J. (2005)	*How to Grow Leaders*	Kogan Page. London
Allender D. (2006)	*Leading with a Limp*	Waterbrook. Colorado Springs
Bacon F. (1990)	*Being a Christian Leader*	Baptist Union GB. Oxford
Bacon F. (1992)	*Church Administration*	Baptist Union GB. Oxford
Baumohl A. (1987)	*Grow Your Own Leaders*	Scripture Union. London
Beasley-Murray P. (1992)	*Radical Believers*	Baptist Union GB. Oxford
Beck A.T. et al (1985)	*Anxiety Disorders and Phobias*	Basic Books. New York
Benware P.N. & Harris B. (1991)	*Leaders in the Making*	Moody Institute. Chicago
Blanchard K. et al (2004)	*Leadership and the One Minute Manager*	Harper Collins. London
Blanchard K. et al (2016)	*Lead like Jesus (Revisited)*	Thomas Nelson. Nashville

Blanchard K. & Broadwell R.(Ed) (2018)	*Servant Leadership in Action*	Berrett-Koehler Pubs. Oakland
Blanchard K. & Miller M. (2014)	*The Secret: What great leaders know and do*	Berrett-Koehler Pubs. Oakland
Boehme R. (1989)	*Leadership for the 21st Century*	Frontline. Seattle
Bolanta T. (2004)	*Mentoring in Life and Ministry*	Restoration Ministries. Nigeria
Bolt P. (2000)	*Coaching for Growth*	Oak Tree Press. Dublin
Bratcher E. et al (1991)	*Mastering Transitions in Ministry*	Multnomah Press. Oregon
Breen M. (2012)	*Multiplying Missional Leaders*	3 D M. Pawleys Island
Buckland C.D. (2006)	*Freedom to Lead*	CWR. Farnham
Burns J. M. (1978)	*Leadership*	Harper & Row. San Francisco
Chalke C. & Relph P. (1995)	*Making a Team Work*	Kingsway. Eastbourne
Childs J. & Pardey D. (2005)	*Mindchange: The power of emotionally intelligent leadership*	Mngmnt Books 2000. Cirencester
Christian Distinctiveness Group (2003)	*Distinctives: The ethos and practice of managing people*	Evangelical Alliance
Clinton Dr J. R. (2012)	*The Making of a Leader, stages of leadership development*	NavPress. Colorado Springs
Clinton T. & Straub J. (2010)	*God Attachment*	Howard Books. New York
Cormack D. (1986)	*Seconds Away*	Marc. Eastbourne
Cormack D. (1987)	*Team Spirit*	Marc. Eastbourne
Cormack D. (1995)	*Change Directions – New ways forward for life, church & business*	Monarch. Crowbridge
Cornwall J. (1988)	*Leaders Eat What You Serve*	Destiny Image Pubs. Pennsylvania
Cousins D. Et al (1990)	*Mastering Church Management*	Mulnomah Press. Oregon

Coventry W.F. & Barker J.L. (1981)	*Management Made Simple*	Heinemann. London
Covey S.R. (1992)	*Principle-Centred Leadership*	Simon & Schuster. London
Covey S.R. et al (1994)	*First Things First*	Simon & Schuster. London
Covey S.R. (2004)	15th Ed *The 7 Habits of Highly Effective People*	Simon & Schuster. London
Covey S.R. (2004)	*The 8th Habit – From effectiveness to greatness*	Simon & Schuster. London
Covey S.R. (2006)	*The Speed of Trust; The one thing that changes everything*	Simon & Schuster. London
Craig N. et al (2015)	*The Discover your True North Fieldbook*	John Wiley & Sons. New Jersey
Crix F. (1991)	*Taking a Lead*	Scripture Union. London
Crossley G. (2008)	*Growing Leaders in the Church*	Evangelical Press. Darlington
Damazio F. (1993)	*Effective Keys to Successful Leadership*	BT Publishing. Oregon
Damazio F. (1994)	*The Vanguard Leader*	BT Publishing. Oregon
Damazio F. & Estes M. (2003)	*Small Group Leader's Handbook*	City Christian Pubs. Portland
Davies G. (1988)	*Stress, the Challenge to Christian Caring*	Kingsway. Eastbourne
Davis F. (2005)	*Leadership in a Nutshell*	Page Free Pubs. Michigan
Dayton E.R. & Engstrom T.W. (1979)	*Strategy for Leadership*	Marc. Bromley
Denton A. (2011)	*Christian Outdoor Leadership*	Smooth Stone Pubs. Fort Collins
DePree M. (1989)	*Leadership is an Art*	Dell Publishing. New York
Dixon R. (1992)	*Management Theory and Practice*	Made Simple Books. Oxford
Donahue B. (2005)	*Jesus – Authentic Leader*	Inter Varsity Press. Illinois

Downey M. (2003)	*Effective Coaching*	Thompson Texere. London
Dulles A. (1976)	*Models of The Church*	Gill & MacMillan. Dublin
Dunn J. (1985)	*The Effective Leader*	Kingsway. Eastbourne
Edwards G. et al (2002)	*Leadership in Management*	Leadership Trust. Ross-on-Wye
Eims L. (1975)	*Be the Leader You were Meant to be*	Victor Books. Illinois
Eims L. (1981)	*Be a Motivational Leader*	Victor Books. Illinois
Elkin P. (1998)	*Mastering Business Planning and Strategy*	Thorogood. London
Engstrom T. W. (1916)	*The Making of a Christian Leader*	Zondervan. Grand Rapids
Farkas C. et al (1997)	*Maximum Leadership 2000*	Orion. London
Fisher R. & Sharp A. (1998)	*Lateral Leadership*	Harper Collins. London
Finney J. (1989)	*Understanding Leadership*	Daybreak. London
Finzel H. (2007)	*The Top Ten Mistakes Leaders Make*	David Cook. Colorado Springs
Garratt B. (2000)	*The Learning Organisation*	HarperCollins. London
Gaukroger S. (1997)	*Battleground: Joshua's strategies for leadership*	Christian Focus Publications
Gibbs E. (2005)	*Leadership Next: Changing leaders in a changing culture*	Inter Varsity Press. Leicester
Gill R. & Burke D. (1996)	*Strategic Church Leadership*	SPCK. London
Gill R. (2001)	*Essays on Leadership*	Leadership Trust. Ross-on-Wye
Gordon B. & Fardouly D. (1990)	*Master Builders: Life & Leadership in the Body of Christ*	Sovereign. Chichester
Greenberger D. & Padesky C.A. (1995)	*Mind over Mood*	Guilford. New York
Greenleaf R.K. (1997)	*Servant Leadership*	Paulist Press. New Jersey

Greenslade P. (2002)	*Leadership: Reflections in Biblical leadership today*	CWR. Farnham
Habecker E. B. (1996)	*Rediscovering the Soul of Leadership*	Victory Books. Illinois
Hacket D. & Martin C.L. (1993)	*Facilitation Skills for Team Leaders*	Crisp. California
Hagberg J.O. & Guelich R.A. (2005)	*The Critical Journey: Stages in the life of faith*	Sheffield Pub Co. Wisconsin
Haggai J. (1986)	*Lead On: Leadership that Endures*	Word Press. Waco
Hain C.W. (1987)	*Learning to Lead*	Inter Varsity Press. Leicester
Handy C. (1991)	*God's of Management*	Arrow Books. London
Handy C. (1993) 4th Edition	*Understanding Organisations*	Penguin. London
Handy C. (1994)	*The Empty Raincoat*	Arrow Books. London
Harari O. (2002)	*The Leadership Secrets of Colin Powell*	McGraw Hill. New York
Hartwig R.T. & Bird W (2015)	*Teams that Thrive: Disciplines of collaborative church leadership*	Inter Varsity Press. Downers Grove
Hayes P. (2011)	*Leading and Coaching Teams to Success*	Open Univ Press. Maidenhead
Heller R. (1998)	*Managing Teams*	Dorling Kindersley. London
Heller R. (1999)	*Effective Leadership*	Dorling Kindersley. London
Heller R. (2002)	*Manager's Handbook*	Dorling Kindersley. London
Hellriegel D. et al (2001) 9th Ed	*Organisational Behaviour*	South Western Coll Pubs. USA
Hesselbein F. et al (1996)	*The Leader of the Future*	Jossey-Bass. San Francisco
Higginson R. (1996)	*Transforming Leadership*	SPCK. London
Honeysett M. (2011)	*Fruitful Leaders: How to make, grow, love and keep them*	Inter Varsity Press. Nottingham
Hughes S. (2001)	*Christ Empowered Living*	CWR. Farnham

Hull B. (1993)	*7 Steps to Transform Your Church*	Baker Bookhouse. Grand Rapids
Hybels B. (1991)	*Church Leaders Handbook*	Willow Creek Assoc. Illinois
Hybels B. (2000)	*Courageous Leadership*	Zondervan. Michigan
Hybels B. et al (2007)	*The Call to Lead: Following Jesus & living out your mission*	Zondervan. Michigan
Irving J.A. & Strauss M.L. (2019)	*Leadership in Christian Perspective*	Baker Academic. Grand Rapids
Irwin D. (Ed) (1998)	*Developing Yourself and Your Staff*	Thorogood. London
Joyner R. (2001)	*Leadership: The power of a creative life*	Morning Star. Charlotte
Kouzes J.M. & Posner B.Z. (2006)	*Christian Reflections on The Leadership Challenge*	Jossey Bass. San Francisco
Lancaster D.B. (2014)	*Training Radical Leaders*	Lightkeeper books. Nashville
Langmuir E. (1969)	*Mountain Leadership*	SSC. Edinburgh
Levicki C. (2002)	*Developing Leadership Genius*	McGraw Hill. Maidenhead
Li C. (2010)	*Open Leadership*	Jossey Bass. San Francisco
Lilley R. (2006)	*Dealing with Difficult People*	Kogan Page. London
Litchfield K. (2006)	*Tend My Flock: Sustaining good pastoral care*	Canterbury Press. Norwich
Lucas B. (2005)	*Discover Your Hidden Talents*	Network Educ Press. Stafford
Mallison J. (1996)	*The Small Group Leader*	Scripture Union. Bletchley
Marshall P. (1998)	*Unlocking Your Potential*	How To Books. Oxford
Marshall R. (2000)	*God @ Work: Discovering the anointing for business*	Destiny Image. Pennsylvania
Marshall T. (1991)	*Understanding Leadership*	Sovereign. Chichester
Matthew S. & Scott K. (1986)	*Leading God's People*	St Andrews Press. Edinburgh

Maxwell J.C. (1993)	*Developing the Leader Within You*	Thomas Nelson Pubs. Nashville
Maxwell J.C. (1995)	*Developing the Leaders Around You*	Thomas Nelson Pubs. Nashville
Maxwell J.C. (1998)	*The 21 Irrefutable Laws of Leadership*	Thomas Nelson Pubs. Nashville
Maxwell J.C. (1999)	*The 21 Indispensible Qualities of a Leader*	Thomas Nelson Pubs. Nashville
Maxwell J.C. (2000)	*The 21 Most Powerful Minutes of a Leader's Day*	Thomas Nelson Pubs. Nashville
Maxwell J.C. (2000)	*Failing Forward – Turning Mistakes into Stepping Stones*	Thomas Nelson Pubs. Nashville
Maxwell J.C. (2001)	*The Right to Lead*	Thomas Nelson Pubs. Nashville
Maxwell J.C. (2001)	*The 17 Indisputable Laws of Teamwork*	Thomas Nelson Pubs. Nashville
Maxwell J.C. (2002)	*Running with the Giants – about life and leadership*	Warner Books. California
Maxwell J.C. (2002)	*The 17 Essential Qualities of a Team Player*	Thomas Nelson Pubs. Nashville
Maxwell J.C. (2002)	*Leadership 101 – What Every Leader needs to Know*	Thomas Nelson Pubs. Nashville
Maxwell J.C. (2003)	*Attitude 101 – What Every Leader Needs to Know*	Thomas Nelson Pubs. Nashville
Maxwell J.C. (2003)	*Equipping 101 – What Every Leader Needs to Know*	Thomas Nelson Pubs. Nashville
Maxwell J.C. (2003)	*Relationships 101 – What Every Leader Needs to Know*	Thomas Nelson Pubs. Nashville
Maxwell J.C. (2004)	*Winning with People*	Thomas Nelson Pubs. Nashville

McFarlin D.B. & Sweeney P.D. (2000)	*Where Egos Dare: The untold truth about narcissistic leaders*	Kogan Page. London
Meadows P. (1988)	*Pressure Points*	Kingsway. Eastbourne
Moody C. (1992)	*Eccentric Ministry: Pastoral Care and Leadership in the Parish*	Darton Longman & Todd. London
Murren D. (1951)	*Leadershift*	Regal Books. California
Munroe M. (1993)	*Becoming a Leader*	Pneuma Life. California
Neighbour R.W. (1995)	*Cell Leader Intern Guidebook:*	Touch Pubs Inc. Houston
Nohria N. & Khurana R. (Ed) (2010)	*Handbook of Leadership Theory and Practice*	Harvard Business Press. Boston
Northouse P.G. (1997)	*Leadership: Theory and Practice*	SAGE. London
Oliver R. (2001)	*Inspirational Leadership*	The Industrial Society. London
Olsson D.L. (1993)	*Church Leaders Handbook*	Willow Creek Ass. Illinois
Osborne L. (2010)	*Sticky Teams: Keeping your Leaders and staff on the same page*	Zondervan. Grand Rapids
Pardy D. (2004)	*Leading Teams*	Inst of Ldrship & Mgemnt. Lichfield
Pardy D. (2007)	*Introducing Leadership*	Elsevier. Oxford
Peck A. (2005)	*Coached by Christ*	CWR. Farnham
Peck A. (2014)	*Coaching and Mentoring*	CWR. Farnham
Perry J. (1983)	*Christian Leadership*	Hodder & Stoughton. London
Person J.B. (1989)	*Cognitive Therapy in Practice*	Norton. New York
Peter L.J. & Hull R. (1969)	*The Peter Principle – why things always go wrong*	Wm Morrow & Co. New York
Phillips J. (1995)	*Only One Life – the biography of Stephen Olford*	Loiseaux. New Jersey
Prime D. (2005)	*Leadership for The Whole Church*	Evangelical Press. Darlington

Prochaska J. & Di Clemente C. (1986)	*Towards a Comprehensive Model of Change*	Springer. New York
Prosser S. (2007)	*To Be a Servant Leader*	Paulist Press. New Jersey
Richardson P. (2004)	*The Life Coach: Become the person you always wanted to be*	Hamlyn. London
Roxburgh A.J. & Romanuk F. (2020)	*The Missional Leader*	Fortress Press. Minneapolis
Rubenstein D. M. (2020)	*How to Lead*	Simon & Schuster. New York
Rusbuldt R.E. (1981)	*Basic Leader Skills: a Handbook for Church Leaders*	Judson Press. Philadelphia
Rush M. (1983)	*Management: a Biblical Approach*	Victor Books. Illinois
Sanders J.O. (1967)	*Spiritual Leadership*	Marshall Pickering. Bromley
Scott S.K. (1998)	*Simple Steps to Impossible Dreams*	Fireside. New York
Sheets D. & Jackson C. (2005)	*Second in Command: Strengthening leaders who serve leaders*	Destiny Image. Shippensburg
Silvoso E. (2002)	*Anointed for Business*	Regal Books. California
Spears L.C. & Lawrence M. (Ed) (2002)	*Focus on Leadership: Servant leadership for the 21st Century*	John Wiley & Sons. New York
Spriggs D. (1993)	*Christian Leadership*	BFBS. Swindon
Stott J.R.W. (2002)	*Calling Christian Leaders*	Inter Varsity Press. Leicester
Thwaites J. (1999)	*The Church Beyond the Congregation*	Paternoster Press. Carlisle
Tidball D. (1986)	*Skilful Shepherds*	Inter Varsity Press. Leicester
Valler P. (2008)	*Get a Life: Winning choices for working people*	Inter Varsity Press. Nottingham
Verwer G. (2019)	*Grace Awakened Leadership*	OM Publishing. London

Viola F. (2008)	*Reimagining Church*	D. Cook. Colorado Springs
Waldock T. & Kelly-Rowat S. (2004)	*The 18 Challenges of Leadership*	Pearson Prentice Hall. Harlow
Warren R. (1995)	*The Purpose Driven Church*	Zondervan. Grand Rapids
White J. (1986)	*Excellence in Leadership*	Inter Varsity Press. Leicester
Williams M.R. (1998)	*Mastering Leadership*	Thorogood Ltd. London
Williams M. (1999)	*Testing Management Skills*	Thorogood. London
Williams N. (1999)	*The Work We Were Born To Do*	Element Books. London
Wright W.C. (2000)	*Relational Leadership: A Biblical model for leadership*	Paternoster. Milton Keynes
Wright W.C. (2005)	*Don't Step on the Rope: Reflections on leadership*	Paternoster. Milton Keynes
Wynne J. (2009)	*Working Without Wilting*	Inter varsity Press. Nottingham
Young J. E. (1990)	*Cognitive Therapy for Personality Disorders*	Prof. Resource Press. Sarasota
Young J. & Klosko J.S. (1994)	*Reinventing Your Life*	Penguin. New York
Youssef M. (1986)	*The Leadership Style of Jesus*	Scripture Press. Amersham
Zeus P. & Skiffington S. (2005)	*The Coaching At Work Tool Kit*	McGraw Hill. Sydney

Appendix A

A Personal Confession of Faith

I believe in God the Father Almighty, maker of heaven and earth and of all things visible and invisible. I believe in one Lord Jesus Christ the only begotten son of God, who was conceived by The Holy Spirit, born in the flesh by a virgin and suffered under Pontius Pilate. He chose death by crucifixion to take upon Himself the full penalty for all my sin. As a result of this, I know that I can receive complete forgiveness and healing in every area of my life.

I believe that after His death and burial He descended into hell, then on the third day, He rose from the dead and ascended into heaven where He sits at the right hand of God, The Father Almighty. I believe that one day He will return in power and glory to judge both the living and the dead and to reign over His eternal kingdom.

I believe in The Holy Spirit who is the very essence of the Father and The Son and who is made available to me to protect and empower me in order that I might become a supernatural ambassador for God in today's world.

I choose to acknowledge, Jesus, that You are my Saviour and my Lord. I repent of, and renounce, all the ways in which I have let you down and not lived according to the standards set out for me in the Scriptures. I am truly sorry for being such a disappointment to You and I now desire to receive afresh your forgiveness.

Please come into my life through Your Holy Spirit to change me more and more into Your likeness. I believe that I am made in Your very image, Lord, and that Your immeasurable love motivates me to respond to You in this way. I commit to do this by being willing to offer the praise and worship of my heart through acts of obedience and service to You every day from now on.

I ask You Lord to cleanse me from everything that is not of You. Please take out of my life the dirt and grime of this world and replace it with all the amazing qualities of Your Holy Spirit. Please enable me, from now on, to live for Your glory and honour alone by walking with You in Holiness and Righteousness all my days. I want to become a positive blessing to every person with whom I come into contact and to radiate Your love and grace in every situation.

Father God, I ask You to do all of this in, and through, the precious name of Jesus Christ, my Lord and my Saviour,

Amen.

TRS/CC/05/15

Appendix B

The Roman Road to Christian Living

(One example from the book of Romans, in The Bible)
**How to move from darkness to light, from death
to life and from bondage to freedom.**

1.   **We are all sinners**   Romans 3 v 9 - 23
     Recognise that no-one is any better than anyone else

2.   **We all deserve death**   Romans 6 v 23
     Acknowledge the consequences of your sinfulness

3.   **We will all be Judged**   Romans 2 v 5 - 12
     Know that God is completely fair and impartial

4.   **We need to repent for sins**   Romans 2 v 4
     Realise the prompting of God's kindness and patience

5.   **God has paid our debt**   Romans 5 v 6 - 8
     Understand how God demonstrated His love for you

6.   **Have faith in Jesus**   Romans 3 v 22 - 26
     Choose to trust in God's promised righteousness

7.   **Receive Peace and Joy**   Romans 5 v 1 - 5
     Accept the free gifts of God through His Son, Jesus

8.   **Get Baptised**   Romans 6 v 1 - 8
     Take action to follow Jesus in acts of obedience

9.   **Be filled with The Holy Spirit**   Romans 8 v 1 - 16
     Receive God's strength mentally, physically and spiritually

10. **Grow in Faith and Practice**   Romans 12 v 1 – 21
     Live by The Spirit, no longer by the standards of the world

**If you choose to walk with God on a daily
basis you will experience whole
new dimensions of life as you keep responding to His promptings.**
TRS/CC/05/90

Appendix C

GROWTH model for individuals and groups

Identify **G**OAL(S) (What do you want to achieve ?)

Establish by discussion about hopes, dreams, visions, ideals, wishes, thoughts etc. Tie them down very specifically. Create actual and mental pictures and descriptions based on Biblical principles.

Assess **R**EALITY (What is the current situation ?)

Consider the actual circumstances and situations in assessing the likelihood of possible achievement. Discuss resources, finance, equipment, materials etc that would be required. Use the Decision Balance Sheet (DBS).

Review **O**PTIONS (What could be done ?)

Outline existing Strengths, Skills, Abilities, Contacts and Resources. Work through a SWOT analysis. Use the Force Field Analysis Sheet (FFA) to look at all possible pathways going forward.

Action **W**AY FORWARD (How will the issue be tackled ?)

Utilise a clear strategy with action plans, broken down into their smallest constituent parts with manageable steps and time frames. Build in checks and monitoring processes with accountability at every stage.

Develop **T**ACTICS (What approaches will ensure success ?)

Prepare a specific strategy for attacking each step in the process. Plan to make even the breaks and hold-ups constructive times. Build-in periods for advice, relaxation, encouragement and refreshment.

Build **H**ABITS (How will success be maintained ?)

Construct a programme of regular positive activity and thinking, including on-going development that will continue to transform the ways in which all kinds of challenges can be faced in the future. Develop a culture of regular training and connection with like-minded people who will constantly challenge the 'status quo'.

Adapted from Growth Coaching International (Australia)
TRS/CCAM/ 09/16

Appendix D

The Stages of Change Model

This model can be utilised by almost any person or organisation where they appear to be stuck or may be struggling over possible issues of change.

1. Pre-Contemplation Stage. Here it may not even be realised that there is a problem or simply, no-one is able to see the issue as a problem. It requires a sensitive and thorough exploration of the benefits of making a change.
2. Contemplation Stage. A realisation is beginning to dawn that there just might be a problem. The need now is to explore and weigh possible avenues of change even though they may not be ready to implement any of them yet.
3. Determination Stage. A decision has now been made and there is a willingness to begin to tackle the problem in a chosen manner. A clear resolve to change and strong dissatisfaction with the status quo is paramount.
4. Action Stage. Specific SMART goals are now being activated and significant strategies for tackling the problem are now being employed. These are carefully monitored and modified as the work progresses.
5. Maintenance Stage. Support structures, key mechanisms and advice/help lines are put in place to reinforce the progress that is being made, along with some protection measures that will encourage new habits to be developed.
6. Relapse Stage. This is always treated as an important part of the learning process where every failure is broken down and analysed to prevent a similar occurrence. The process can be re-activated at any stage.

Stages of Change Model

Adapted from Prochaska & DiClemente (1986)
"Towards a Comprehensive Model of Change"

Appendix E

Managing your Fitness

Where leaders are not in a traditional Monday to Friday, 9 to 5 job, it can be important for them to develop their own weekly plan to help them maintain a healthy work/life balance. This may be especially important for leaders of churches, Christian organisations, charities and voluntary bodies where they are required to manage their own timetable and where the pressures of the job can often squeeze out family and leisure opportunities.

A typical programme for someone who is a church leader might look something like this:

	9.00 – 12.30pm	2.00 – 5.30pm	7.00 – 10.30pm
Monday	Admin work & prep for the week	Follow up activities	Church Prayer Meeting
Tuesday	Sermon Prep	Pastoral Visiting	Time Off
Wednesday	Church Coffee Bar	Time Off	Elders/Deacons/Leaders meetings
Thursday	Time Off	Hospital Visiting	Church Bible Study
Friday	Parents and Toddlers Group	Time Off	Youth Meeting
Saturday	Time Off	Time Off	Time Off
Sunday	Morning Service	Time Off	Evening Service and Fellowship meeting

Of course, this can be infinitely flexible and will depend very much on the individual role of the person concerned.

Such a programme would allow the leader to spend quality time with his family, to take up other activities or interests, and to socialise outside his work environment. Of course, these are merely guidelines which may not be able to be held rigidly but can give a clear indication of intent.

By breaking the week down into 21 'work periods', it is possible to see the comparative time given to work and family and to build-in specific times for alternative activities.

As a general principle, a full working week is considered to consist of five and a half days, or 11 'work periods'. That means there could be 10 periods each week which the leader is able to allocate for his leisure and pleasure.

TRS/CC/03/85

Other Publications by the same Author

A small series of A5 full colour booklets aimed at helping people towards Spiritual Maturity entitled "**Gateway to Life**"

1. Fundamentals
2. Moving Forward
3. Breaking Free
4. Understanding The Holy Spirit
5. Exploring Worship
6. Christian Paradoxes
7. Spiritual Maturity

All available from the website: www.gateway-to-life.info

"Christian Parallels"
A book which explores the similarities between learning to ski and living the Christian life.

ISBN: 978-1-913247-60-7

Published by Kingdom Publishers, Enfield, UK.
Widely available through bookshops, Amazon, etc.

"Becoming a Christian Counsellor"
A book for everyone who is interested in, or might benefit from, counselling.
It addresses many of the problems people ascribe to counselling and gives a comprehensive outline of a Christian approach that can be used with people of any faith or of none.

ISBN: 978-1-6642-3993-7

Published by WestBow Press, Bloomington Indiana, USA
Widely available through bookshops, Amazon, etc.

Printed in Great Britain
by Amazon

24691715R10099